wor

PIO
OR
SETTLERS?

Exodus: Adventurous faith for today

PHILIP MOHABIR

Scripture Union
130 City Road, London EC1V 2NJ

First published 1991
by Scripture Union, 130 City Road,
London EC1V 2NJ

British Library Cataloguing in Publication Data

Mohabir, Philip
Pioneers or Settlers?
1. Bible. OT. Exodus. Christianity. Scriptures.
I. Title II. Series
222.1206

ISBN 0 86201 635 5

Phototypeset by Intype, London
Printed and bound by Cox & Wyman Ltd, Reading.

CONTENTS

ABOUT THE AUTHOR

Philip Mohabir was born in 1937 into a Hindu family in British Guiana, and into a community employed on a sugar plantation. It was during a Religious Education class at school that Philip first heard Jesus' call to follow him. God further called him to go to England as a missionary.

Philip arrived in London in 1956 to discover a great rift between black and white Christians. He was himself excluded by white Christians from worshipping with them, because of his colour. His concern to see the healing of this rift has led him to pioneer a work of reconciliation between black and white Christians, Asians and Afro-Caribbeans.

In 1984 Philip founded the West Indian Evangelical Alliance and now travels around the world, preaching and working for racial reconciliation and social justice, and planting churches. He and his wife, Muriel, have six daughters.

ACKNOWLEDGEMENTS

My sincere gratitude goes to my dear wife Muriel, without whose encouragement I could not have done this work. Thanks also to Becky Totterdell who had enough confidence for both of us, and to Gerald Coates for letting me use as the book's title a phrase that has been associated with his ministry for many years. I shall always remain grateful to Cathy and Peter who constantly made room and place to push me on. I would also like to thank Maggie Fielden, for her help with statistical research. Finally to my daughters, my son-in-law Tim to whom I owe so much but especially to David who made it possible for Anne to spend many days typing and reading the manuscript. A special tribute goes to Anne.

Philip Mohabir
London

INTRODUCTION

Contemporary society is in urgent need of renewal. If we are to avert total moral collapse and spiritual bankruptcy then we must rediscover sound moral and spiritual values and return to a lifestyle which reflects true freedom and God's order.

Exodus is an exciting account of God's love and care for a people who were poor and powerless, a people who had lost their way in Egypt, and their sense of community. But God powerfully brought them out of their bondage, then faithfully and patiently recreated them into a community. He moulded them into a new nation and gave them a context within which they could love and serve one another. From their experiences, we can learn essential values and important principles which can be of great comfort and inspiration to us in the 1990s.

In this book we will look only at selected parts of Exodus. But, through those, we will discover that the highlights of Israel's pilgrimage with God can be the highlights of our own experience, too. They are:

- Committing themselves to a covenant relationship with God.
- God's direct intervention in the everyday affairs of people.
- The manifestation of the supernatural power of God

released on behalf of his people and against those who oppose them.

- God's care and provision even when his people are undeserving.
- The patience of God as he carefully sought to reconstruct them into a unit – community and nation – to be an alternative society.
- The design of God to draw his people into an ever-increasing intimacy in fellowship, through the building of the tabernacle, and in equipping them to be a prophetic people.

Great love, great power, great provision, great care, great faithfulness, great foundations – all to one end: great freedom and fellowship.

I have tried to draw out some lessons which may be applicable to our generation, with the sincere desire that we, too, might find new hope and dare to trust in God to bring us out of our bondage and difficulties, that we may enjoy living in relationship and sweet fellowship with our Father.

This book is not meant to be a treatise or a comprehensive document on Exodus but rather to act as a reminder to stimulate our faith, inspire our confidence, and warn us of mistakes to avoid. I humbly pray that all who read the thoughts expressed in these pages will be comforted and challenged to be all God wants them to be and never be content to live below God's best for them.

1

GOD'S ULTIMATE

Why am I here? Is there any real purpose or meaning to life? Am I just an accident? What am I trying to achieve in life? These questions have probably crossed your mind at some time. How did you answer them? Exodus gives some exciting, awe-inspiring answers. It speaks of God's plan for each individual and for humankind as a whole, a plan conceived and designed in love; a plan that is best for you.

God's ultimate purpose for you is that your whole life should be a celebration; a celebration of God:

> 'Let my people go that they may celebrate *ME*.'
>
> *Exodus 5:1, NASB.*

God longs to see all people return to his divine ownership. He longs to make us his precious possession for whom he is solely responsible and over whom he rules. We are to be a kingdom people serving as priests and prophets to the nations (Exodus 19:6); a prophetic people reflecting Christ.

Exodus is an action-packed thriller! Its central themes are God's unfailing love and care for his people, and his ability to rescue them from the most desperate conditions. God is able to deliver, 'he is able to save completely' (Hebrews 7:25). God's intention for each of us always was, and still is, that we should *reign in life*, enjoy life to the full. He created us in his own image and likeness to be happy, healthy, productive and to rule in all of life's ups and downs.

WHO AM I?

In Egypt, the Israelites lost all sense of identity. They were simply cogs in a brick-making machine, devalued, deprived of respect and even the most basic of human rights. There are times when we feel something of their despair in our own lives. When we are rejected by those we are working for, insulted, taken for granted, abused – we begin to wonder who we are. Our sense of identity evaporates. We feel like so much rubbish, worthless and useless.

Genesis clearly states that we are God's creation and the crowning glory of all his creative activity:

> 'Then God said, "Let us make man in our image, in our likeness, and let them rule over the fish of the sea and the birds of the air, over the livestock, over all the earth, and over all the creatures that move along the ground."
>
> So God created man in his own image,

> in the image of God he created him;
> male and female he created them.
>
> God blessed them and said to them, "Be fruitful and increase in number; fill the earth and subdue it. Rule over the fish of the sea and the birds of the air and over every living creature that moves on the ground." ' *Genesis 1:26–28*

Humankind is a thing of exquisite beauty, unsurpassed in wisdom and intelligence, fearfully and wonderfully made. Created by God for God. Delightful and delicate. A marvel to the angels, a target to the devil and a subject of much controversy to unbelieving people who are so intellectual that they have become incapable of any true intelligence. They would like to make monkeys out of us! Nonsense! Such intricate precision simply cannot have happened by chance. There was, rather, a brilliant mind at work, carefully planning the origin, nature and purpose of humankind. God said 'Let us make man . . .' (Genesis 1: 26–28).

Four facts about who we are, are highlighted in these verses from Genesis:

1 Our distinctiveness

We are different from the rest of creation. We are not like the birds or bees, plants or animals. Although there may be biological similarities, we are not one and the same with the rest of creation. We are not the end product of some evolutionary process. We are not freaks. We were created, male and female, in God's own image and likeness.

2 Our equality

We were created to be equals of one another not one superior to the other. Yet each of us is also unique. Though in many ways different from each other, we are all created in the image of God.

3 Our personhood

Being created 'in God's image' clearly implies that God imparted to us something of his very own person. Unlike the rest of creation, we were created to feel, think and act as God would. God gave us intelligence, emotions, will and spirituality. He built into us the value and dignity peculiar only to himself. Just think of it, we are not just animals or biological products but people, a product of rare and precious value, the work of God's own hands! Any system, institution, law, action or person that detracts from that or decreases the value of people, not only robs them of their dignity but transgresses their human rights. Such action is in direct conflict with God's purposes for his creation and so places the one who degrades another into conflict with God. To touch his creation is to touch his image, his person.

4 Our immortality

God endowed us with immortality. That is, the life we have is not only different from that of the animals but there is an eternal quality to it. This is the reason why human life is so sacred. We do not just die and rot. We are more than physical bodies, we are also soul and spirit.

When God created mankind he made sure that it was very good, perfect in every way, lacking nothing, deficient in no aspect. Man and woman were totally whole, complete in every way. They were created in God's image to rule over the earth and to enjoy a full and complete life. We were created uniquely beautiful and beautifully unique. A work of unsurpassed excellence, intelligence and innocence. Exquisite! We were destined for greatness, goodness and freedom. God's ultimate goal for us is to be persons like himself, full of harmony, joy, justice; free from all fears, pressures and tensions, pain and hurts; without defects or deficiencies. Genesis 1:28 sums it up: 'God blessed them and said to them, "Be fruitful and increase in number; fill the earth and subdue it." ' He intended us to be free and whole, and to reign with him.

So what went wrong?

PARADISE INVADED

We need to go back to Genesis 3 to find out. Here we are told that our garden paradise was invaded by an enemy. Through Adam and Eve's disobedience, sin entered into our beautiful world. The garden became a place of thorns, thistles, shame and disgrace. We got ourselves truly messed up. Paul explains what happened when he writes that it was through the disobedience of one man that sin entered into the world (Romans 5:19). As a result we lost all contact with God and, with him, our sense of direction and purpose. Our sense of values was irreparably damaged, our dignity severely injured. We blew it. This was a tragedy of enormous proportions and carried with it very serious consequences. Sin came in and God went out, and so did joy, peace, love, kindness, harmony, justice. 'We all, like sheep, have gone astray, each of us has turned to his own way' (Isaiah 53:6). Everything God intended for the human race went haywire.

By the entrance of sin Satan threw a spanner in the works. It was as though somebody had changed all the price tags: our priorities and value systems got hopelessly confused, our perspectives in life terribly mixed up. A virus had got into the computer programme and the human race was experiencing a disastrous malfunction. The door was opened wide for Satan to walk right into our lives. He has wreaked havoc: lies, deception, murder, hate, selfishness, pride; absolute chaos and disaster. Catastrophe with a capital C. We see it all around us. Alienated from our Father, we are helpless victims of a ruthless enemy.

It was always God's intention for people so wonderfully, beautifully and carefully created to be in harmony with him and enjoy intimate fellowship, a love relationship that was strong. To be at peace with God. All this was now forfeited. The children of Israel in the land of Egypt, under the might and domination of the Pharaohs, are a picture of the whole human race. By Adam's disobedience we were sold into sin and became captives to Satan. The conditions described for us in the opening chapters of Exodus mirror the condition of all mankind. Satan has vowed to frustrate God's purposes for mankind and Jesus exposed this aim when he said 'the thief comes only to steal and kill and destroy' (John 10:10).

ENTER: JESUS

God's original intention for us – to mirror his beauty and excellence, to reign over all that God created – was now frustrated. But this is not the end of the story! When all seemed totally hopeless and lost Jesus entered the scene, just as God sent Moses to the children of Israel. Jesus came to restore all that was lost, to redeem humankind totally and reconcile us fully to God. Now it is again possible for all people to enjoy a relationship with God, know him as Father and experience the warmth of his love. In Romans 5 Paul says that, 'by the transgression of one man [Adam], death reigned through that one, but now through the abundance of grace we will reign in life through the one, Jesus Christ' (Romans 5:17, NASB). In verse 18 he continues, 'through one transgression condemnation came upon all men, but through the death of Christ freedom from all guilt and condemnation is given to all men.' In verse 19 he concludes, 'Through one man's disobedience many were made sinners, even so, through the obedience of the one, Jesus, many were made righteous, for where sin increased and abounded the grace of God through Jesus abounded even all the more.'

Jesus came to deliver us, just as Moses was used by God to be the deliverer for the children of Israel from the bondage and slavery of Pharaoh. Jesus, our champion, saviour and deliverer has come, conquered the devil and has broken all the chains of our captivity that we might go free from death, condemnation and bondage to all the awful things which the devil has worked into our lives and society. Paul explained it to the Colossians by saying, 'He has rescued us from the dominion of darkness and brought us into the kingdom of the Son he loves' (Colossians 1:13). We have literally been moved out of one sphere into another, one realm to another, one state to another. Now, once again, we can experience the rule of God, enjoy his presence, receive his peace, reach out and up for our full potential in God and fulfil all his purposes for our lives.

This can become a reality when we reach out in faith and accept all that Christ died to give us. 'God's ear is not heavy nor his hands short that he cannot hear us and reach us and help us. However, our sins and our rebellion have hid his face from us and separated us from God' (Isaiah 59:1–2, NASB). God, in his holiness and justice, could not ignore our sin, yet out of his love for us he wanted to reach out and draw us back to himself. That is why God intervened to provide a way out. His rescue plan was not an afterthought; God deliberately planned that, through Jesus Christ, he would free us from the desperate state in which we were and deliver us from our captors.

It is God's desire that we live our daily lives out of a sense of our 'throne' position in creation, now restored to us in Jesus; a life that reflects the integrity, dignity and power of God. Rather than being slaves and victims, we are intended to reign and, out of the authority of the throne, overcome those things that attack, assail and subject us.

So, the conditions of oppression and affliction in which we find the people of Israel do not reflect God's heart for humanity. Far from it. That is why God intervened to restore them to their original status, rights and riches.

God did not forget Israel, neither does he ever give

up on us. He does not turn his back on us even when we rebel and walk away from him; his desire is always to restore us fully to our right to rule in life, to regain all we have lost – our position, our dignity, our value as human beings and, most of all, our relationship with him. God never created us to be slaves to sin, never created us to be controlled and dominated by circumstances, to be pressured by the difficulties and adversities of life. We were created to be victors not victims, conquerors not the conquered. 'We who were once lost, now by grace are saved and made to sit on the throne with Jesus and out of that throne position we should now live and act out our new creation life' (Ephesians 2:6–7, NASB). Romans 5:8 says, 'While we were still sinners, Christ died for us.' Anyone who accepts Jesus now by faith, and makes him Lord of his or her life, is a 'new creation'. Therefore, now we should live and act out our new creation life. Reigning in life is our true destiny, always was and still is.

Finally, Romans 8:29 says that God desires we should be like his Son Jesus. Why? Because he is the perfect likeness of God in whose image we were created. God is Father, Son and Holy Spirit. God's desire is that we should be restored to his likeness, by faith, by the work of the Holy Spirit and by yielding ourselves to the Lordship of Christ. It is the heart cry of God for each of us to enjoy all that fullness of life in Christ: abundant, overflowing life.

God's ultimate goal for us is that his Son's image be planted deep within our own beings. Whatever is marred, deficient, weak, bankrupt and poverty-ridden in our lives, Christ, through the Holy Spirit can turn it around. He can make the marred whole, the deficient full, the weak strong and the poor rich, through making us like Jesus.

It should always be our prayer, therefore, to reach our full potential in God, where each one of us is unique. God designed us to do so, and has a glorious future, a useful and meaningful purpose for each of us. We should not settle for *good*, we should go for *best*! Never accept mediocrity when excellence beckons you. God has given you the capacity to reach for the stars – go for it! Expand your vision and see that you are capable of higher and better things by faith in Christ. You can do it!

2

TRAPPED!

Through no fault of your own, you find yourself locked into a situation, boxed in on every side. Imprisoned with no way out. Trapped!

It can sometimes seem as though someone has deliberately manoeuvered every circumstance and orchestrated events around us with the sole purpose of making us thoroughly miserable. Any attempt to escape only makes matters worse; we are only further frustrated. We feel used and manipulated for the pleasure of others. It's frightening and hopeless, a rough deal.

This was exactly the situation with the people of Israel in Egypt. Through no fault of their own they were trapped in the machinations of an evil system, oppressed by a cruel and heartless tyrant. Their burdens were increased day by day as they were mercilessly exploited:

'These are the names of the sons of Israel who entered Egypt with Jacob, each with his family: Reuben, Simeon, Levi and Judah; Issachar, Zebulun and Benjamin; Dan and Naphtali; Gad and Asher. The descendants of Jacob numbered seventy in all; Joseph was already in Egypt.

Now Joseph and all his brothers and all that generation died, but the Israelites were fruitful and multiplied greatly and became exceedingly numerous, so that the land was filled with them.

Then a new king, who did not know about Joseph, came to power in Egypt. "Look," he said to his people, "the Israelites have become much too numerous for us. Come, we must deal shrewdly with them or they will become even more numerous and, if war breaks out, will join our enemies, fight against us and leave the country."

So they put slave masters over them to oppress them with forced labour, and they built Pithom and Rameses as store cities for Pharaoh. But the more they were oppressed, the more they multiplied and spread; so the Egyptians came to dread the Israelites and worked them ruthlessly. They made their lives bitter with hard labour in brick and mortar and with all kinds of work in the fields; in all their hard labour the Egyptians used them ruthlessly.'

Exodus 1:1–14

HOW DID THEY COME TO BE TRAPPED?

It all began with Joseph, the youngest of Jacob's twelve sons. Joseph seemed to go from one trap to another, sometimes through his own fault, sometimes through no fault of his own. But his story introduces us to a God who springs traps open and draws his people out into freedom and richer service.

Jacob and his sons were pastoral people and had large flocks of sheep. Joseph's brothers were hard working men who tended their father's flocks, and they were jealous of Joseph to the point of insanity because he was their father's favourite son. So they conspired to get rid of him. They trapped him, sold him to traders who were on the way to Egypt, then faked his death. They knew Joseph would be sold by those traders as a slave into Egypt. Joseph was the victim of a wicked scheme hatched in the bosom of his own brothers, his family, those closest to him.

Upon arrival in Egypt, he was duly sold to Potiphar, the chief of Pharaoh's bodyguards – trapped again. But God came to his rescue in that situation, so that everything he did was progressive and prosperous. Potiphar felt so secure in Joseph's ability to manage that he entrusted all the affairs of his household into his capable hands.

Potiphar was a man of some considerable wealth and influence and was married to a real Egyptian beauty. She could not believe that any man would not find her desirable. She wanted Joseph to be her lover but he was not interested. He would not sin against his employer or against God, nor would he take advantage of a woman's weakness. Having failed to seduce him, she threw caution to the wind and made a bold attempt to grab him by his garment and force herself on him. But he fled out of the house and out of that trap. But in the process he left part of his garment in her hand.

Frustrated and realising she would never succeed, she framed him, seeking to avenge herself. He was discredited, dishonoured and spent several years locked up in prison. Trapped again! This time, through doing nothing but good! Joseph could easily have sat in prison, languishing in self pity, mourning his many misfortunes. Who would blame him? First the conspiracy of his brothers, then the conniving of a lustful woman, now a prison sentence for a crime he did not commit – it would have been so easy to justify himself and spend his years getting depressed. No. Instead, he dared to believe for better things and made himself useful, serving his fellow prisoners with distinction. He was an outstanding example even in adversity, a testimony of God's presence and grace at work in his life.

But God sprang the trap again. In prison he had interpreted the dream of a fellow prisoner, the cup-bearer of the king. As that dream had indicated, the cup-bearer was reinstated. Then the king himself had a very distressing dream and no one could be found in all of Pharaoh's empire who could interpret it. Then the cup-bearer remembered Joseph. He was brought out, proved to be the only man in the whole empire who could interpret the King's dream, and was promptly appointed Prime Minister. The dream had predicted seven years of famine and, by his inspiration and wise management, Joseph prepared the nation to face it and so saved them from a great disaster.

The famine spread throughout Egypt and the nations about. Jacob and his family were also affected. His sons went in search of food and eventually came to Egypt to buy food from Pharaoh's store. They had no idea that their brother, Joseph, whom they had sold years back and assumed was dead, was the minister in charge of this operation. Nor would they have imagined in their wildest dreams that he had become the second man in the kingdom. A slave elevated to such heights of power and authority? But Joseph knew them when they arrived. Yet, instead of arresting his brothers, punishing them or seeking revenge for their evil deed, Joseph forgave them. He welcomed and embraced them. When they realised who the Prime Minister was, they were convinced they were done for. Trapped! But through Joseph's influence Pharaoh granted them freedom to settle in Egypt and prosper. An alien, immigrant people was given a home.

EGYPT: A PLACE OF SAFETY?

Egypt was for many years an extensive empire. The dynasty of the Pharaohs dominated the world's political, social and economic scene for generations. It was advanced in the arts, music, education and military skills and was the world's centre of trade and commerce. It had a sophisticated system of government and enjoyed a high quality of life. The grandeur and splendour of Egypt's courts and the palaces of its rulers were second to none and the envy of all. Situated on the north-eastern coast of Africa, it was constantly refreshed and nourished by the waters of the mighty Nile. The fertile delta and plains of the Nile stretched for thousands of square miles and provided lush pastures and many square miles of alluvial soil suitable for agriculture.

Recent archaelogical excavations tell us of the riches, splendour and glory of an ancient era. As researchers delve more deeply into Egyptian antiquity, their cities, chariots, pageantries, rituals, processions and leisure activities reveal a highly developed and sophisticated culture. Egyptian women were renowned for their flamboyant clothes, hairstyles and painted faces. They were a polytheistic people and freely indulged in idol worship. Pre-eminent among their many pagan forms of worship and practice was the worship of the bull calf, a symbol of fertility and prosperity. The figure was usually carved out of wood, then plated either with silver or gold. Much of their wealth was booty from the conquest and oppression of other peoples. Their gains were accumulated by unjust and corrupt exploitation, their cities and great palaces built on the blood, sweat and tears of captive slaves. Their exploitation and extortion knew no limit and showed no mercy. They plundered whole nations and cultures to build and maintain their own.

TRAPPED BY A WEALTHY SOCIETY

Joseph died and with the passage of time the successors to the throne forgot the immense contribution that he and his generation had made to the nation. They began to view them with suspicion, as 'foreigners' still, an alien people. After four hundred years and twenty generations they still could not trust them to be patriotic. They saw them as a threat to their safety. Once their most valuable asset, now they were seen as a drain on the economy. Motivated by suspicion and fear, imagined or real, the Egyptian government proceeded to vigorously oppress the Hebrew people, the very people who still contributed such a great deal to the life of the nation. How long must one live, pay taxes and labour in a country before one qualifies for, or is considered worthy of, citizenship? In this case four hundred years was obviously not long enough. Rough justice! Israel was trapped in a situation from which there seemed no escape.

Pharaoh oppressed and afflicted the children of Israel. It all started with jealousy. He could not live with the thought that the children of Israel could be free to be themselves, to prosper, run their own lives, care for their own families, bring up their children in the way they wanted, have their own lands and pursue their own futures. Pharaoh and his advisors became jealous of the Hebrews simply because they were an industrious, hard working and progressive people.

Note the different steps here. They grew jealous, then they felt threatened. They could not handle their own fears, jealousies and insecurities, so they proceeded to oppress the children of Israel. Pharaoh took away their freedom to come and go as they pleased and designed ways to keep the people under control.

One way to keep them under control was to demoralise them by giving them the worst jobs, that no one else in society wanted. And to prevent them organising protest marches and 'causing trouble', Pharaoh made sure the physical demands of the work were so rigorous, and the punishment for not doing it so total, that no one would have the energy to complain.

To make the bricks for Pharaoh's storage houses and palaces meant trampling mud and straw mixed with water and limestone in large pits. Then the mixture had to be neatly shaped and carefully stacked for firing in kilns. Only high quality bricks were acceptable and to produce high quality bricks the texture must be just right. To get the right texture meant hours upon hours of knee deep, bare feet trampling. Tramp, tramp, tramp, day in, day out, tramp, tramp. Under the intense heat of the Egyptian sun, and in high, dense humidity, this gruelling activity continued on and on. Many grew weary and tired. Many aged considerably before their time. Others fell hopeless victims to sickness and disease. Many died. Those who survived lost all hope, their hearts had long since died within them. Those clay pits must have been hated. Not only were they the bane of their waking hours but the scene of their nightmares. The task masters were never satisfied. They always demanded more by increasing their production targets. With every passing day they introduced more schemes to make their burdens even more intolerable. The spiritual parallels are not hard to find: once the devil has us in his grip he does not give us an easy life.

As they trampled in those pits, knee deep in the mud, straw, grime and dirt, the Hebrews must have felt their own self worth and dignity being trampled under the giant feet of unscrupulous men. They were a people dispossessed, demoralised and humiliated to the extreme. They were the 'nobodies' in society, a non people, an invisible minority group not even considered worthy of second-class citizenship. They were just things to be controlled, used and manipulated. They had no political voice and were denied all civil and human rights. They were reduced to an existence of mere survival and were confined to a reservation – a slave encampment under strict surveillance and policing. Their movements being restricted, they were made to work long and hard hours to meet the production quotas set by the foremen. The women were abused, their chastity violated to gratify the whims and fancies of their masters. Can you imagine their humiliation? Even the joy of having a baby boy became a terrible crime. To have a son was forbidden:

> 'The king of Egypt said to the Hebrew midwives, whose names were Shiphrah and Puah, "When you help the Hebrew women in childbirth and observe them on the delivery stool, if it is a boy, kill him; but if it is a girl, let her live." The midwives, however, feared God and did not do what the king of Egypt had told them to do; they let the boys live. Then the king of Egypt summoned the midwives and asked them, "Why have you done this? Why have you let the boys live?"
>
> The midwives answered Pharaoh, "Hebrew women are not like Egyptian women; they are vigorous and give birth before the midwives arrive."
>
> So God was kind to the midwives and the people increased and became even more numerous. And because the midwives feared God, he gave them families of their own.
>
> Then Pharaoh gave this order to all his people: "Every boy that is born you must throw into the river, but let every girl live." ' *Exodus 1:15–22*

This must be among the first records of genocide, the mass murder of helpless human beings. It's certainly not the last. The spirit of infanticide is still alive and at large.

Credulity is stretched to its limit, just to think that any sane, intelligent human being can advance a theory and devise the means necessary to murder thousands of innocent children. When is a life not a life? Does it really matter if they are six or thirty-six weeks old? When is the deliberate taking of life not murder? When it is legalised! To justify and sanction such drastic action in such an advanced and civilised society is simply beyond comprehension. It is murder. The Egyptian rulers murdered the innocent babies of a weak and defenceless people. Who did they use to do their dirty work? The midwives – their health service. The passage of time and progress of human development have not been able to drown the voice of the Hebrew children. So much for the sacredness of human life.

If it was possible to ask the Egyptians for a rationale for their behaviour, the answer they would give would be something like this. They have no right to live in our land, why don't they go home? They are becoming too mighty, there are too many of them, they threaten our own economic prosperity. We can't trust their motives nor can we depend on their patriotism. They are a threat to our defence. Their presence is a constant embarrassment and undermines our quality of life. Our own culture will be under seige if this is allowed to continue. Who knows where it will end? A stop must be put to these people. Something must be done before it is too late.

What prejudice! What an attitude! How ridiculous, that a defenceless and harmless people should pose such a tremendous problem to the greatest nation on earth; the most powerful military might of its day terrified by an immigrant, alien people. They were so obsessed by their increasing numbers that the threat was grossly exaggerated and blown out of all proportion. The Hebrews were perceived to be a problem rather than a resource. Pharaoh was prepared to commit genocide in order to preserve the rights of the indigenous population from the perceived threat of a hard-working, unarmed, beleagered people who made enormous contributions throughout many generations to the wealth and prosperity of the nation. How unjust! How crazy! Egypt with all its riches, art, culture and military might was so gripped by fear that, instead of exploring ways and means by which these people could have been further accommodated, instead of initiating plans and programmes by which the nation could be enriched and enhanced by their diversity, he planned for their extinction.

Egypt's social philosophy was purely utilitarian: accommodate people as long as they are useful and needed. Get rid of them when they are no longer convenient or have outlived their usefulness. Discard them on the rubbish heap.

It would seem that not much has changed with the passage of time. There are many parallels today in our contemporary society. We may not see the severe whip of Pharaoh's task masters but the same spirit and forces that were working then are actively at work now in twentieth-century Britain. The means and methods may be different but they produce the same debilitating and dehumanising effect on men and women. Where people feel threatened by immigrant communities, they still devise means whereby they can use the less privileged and exploit them to further their own cause. Through oppression – the clever use of systems, institutions, financial programmes and laws – they serve their own vested interests. Like Pharaoh, they soon forget the service and the value that these people gave in the past. Heartlessly and mercilessly they are prepared to go to any lengths in order to preserve their own selfish life-style and to feather their own nests. The heart of man has not changed very much. Right in our society, in our cities, in our villages, we find men and women who are enduring such oppression.

The church cannot ignore these injustices. It must have a prophetic voice and be God's agent to bring about change in every age, among every people and in every country. Injustice is sin; it must be repented of and condemned.

TRAPPED IN OURSELVES

The heart of the story in Exodus is of an oppressed, enslaved people held in bondage by a merciless tyrant, who were led to freedom by Moses. Similarly, the chains that hold us in bondage can be broken by the power of God. There are many instances in our own lives where we need the delivering power of God. Jesus said, 'he who the Son of man sets free is free indeed' (John 8:36, NASB). Jesus is our Moses who can set us free from the oppression and bondage in our own lives. Secular society is our Egypt, and Satan and his demons act towards us as Pharaoh and his task masters.

Bondage is anything which restricts us and prevents us from being totally free in our thoughts, choices and actions. It is that something which holds us and drives us to do things that we know are wrong, yet cannot help ourselves doing. True freedom is the ability to be able to say 'no'. 'No' to our friends, to our cravings and to our addictions. Many people boast of being free and yet, deep within them, they are slaves to their own traditions, religious and cultural forms, racial prejudices, class systems and sexist views. To be in bondage is to be held in involuntary servitude to a person or a thing, attitude or action. Some are compelled to act against their own good sense and will. It is the state of being controlled by an external influence or power. In other words, 'being hooked'.

Some people are trapped by certain habits. No amount of reason can shift them. They seem blind to reason. They are held in a syndrome out of which they cannot climb or break loose. Others form unhealthy relationships that do nothing to contribute to their quality of life. People cannot back away even from relationships that are obviously destructive. Some form alliances, indulge in illicit sexual affairs and immoral practices. They are slaves, against all their better judgement. Some people get involved with third parties who threaten their own marriage and the happiness of their family. Yet they persist. We are bound by things, people and habits that ruin our sense of decency and cause so much pain. We know it! We regret our plight but cannot resist or break the hold. This is bondage. It is slavery. It puts chains on our mind, sense of values, emotions and will. These are chains which only Jesus can break.

Emotional ties can be so strong that people become possessive and jealous to the point of insanity. Lust and uncontrollable desires hold people captive, even though they bring a lot of heartache and pain. Lust for power, money, status, sex and prestige drive people to pursue them at the cost of health and happiness, friends and family. People become trapped by their own perceptions of life, creating images that are unjust and unreal. But they would rather hold on to their stereotypes and judge everyone from their own framework, than break out of their self made prisons to embrace a wider view of life or accommodate another opinion.

Other aspects of bondage are more deeply rooted in our own personalities: unfounded fears, a spirit of rejection, a sense of inadequacy, low self esteem, self indulgence, injustice, an unforgiving spirit and habits which cling to us like leeches. Some are afraid to live, others are afraid to die. People are afraid of failure, other people's opinions, others' assessment of us. There are people who are even afraid of their own shadows, afraid to face the darkness, the dawning of a new day, afraid of the past and afraid of the future.

Fear torments, and brings with it misery which eventually leads to nervous breakdowns. But perfect love casts out fear. Jesus, in the Gospels, often encouraged and sometimes rebuked his disciples with these words: 'Don't be afraid.' Don't be afraid of the anxieties and pressures of life; don't be afraid in the midst of an angry, stormy sea; don't be afraid of the future. 'Don't be afraid', Jesus said again and again as he ministered to his disciples. Not even in the face of death or the grave. Not even in the face of seeming impossibilities, for all things are possible with God.

Are you feeling trapped, imprisoned, locked in? See, Jesus stands at the door of your heart and knocks. Will you open the door of life and bid him enter? He will lead you out into glorious liberty and freedom.

One person's story

The story of Israel and their deliverance might seem to be in the distant past. You may wonder if it bears any relevance to you. It worked for them in those days but does God do things like that today? Is God interested in individuals today? In my situation, for example?

* * *

She was a demure, beautiful, black teenager; dark hair, sparkling brown eyes – a stunning beauty, full of hope and future. Mum and Dad were poor and had to work long and arduous hours just to survive, but the stresses and strains of modern life caused the marriage to break up. The daughter was thrown out into the street. She imbibed its culture and practices. Driven by loneliness, encouraged and challenged by her peers she drifted into drugs and then petty crime and eventually violence. She was so intoxicated with the exhilaration and pleasure that these things brought that she did not stop to consider the hurt, pain and damage she was accumulating for herself. The euphoria of the moment carried her like a swift flowing stream without any consideration of tomorrow. Life was one big party. She was barely sixteen.

Then the inevitable happened. One day, she and her friends ran into problems with the police. She was arrested, convicted and sentenced to prison. Her friends deserted her, no one seemed to care. Her prison cell became her home, her only companion its bare trappings. She was lonely and depressed as days turned into weeks, weeks into months. Her prison cell began to close in on her and the stark reality of her situation gradually dawned on her. Then, reluctantly, she began to read the little New Testament left her by some visitor. Slowly she began to think. Could this Jesus also help *me* out of *my* predicament? He healed the sick, raised the dead, befriended publicans, sinners and outcasts in society. He changed the woman of Samaria and Mary Magdalen. Could he help *me*? Eventually, she summoned up her courage and in desperation cried out to Jesus. To her surprise, she experienced a gentle, soft presence of the Lord penetrating the cold dismal prison cell, dispelling her fears. She felt that her sins were now forgiven, the guilt and condemnation washed away. Gone! An overwhelming peace flooded her heart as in successive waves the love of God washed over her. Her inner self warmed with an assurance that God accepted her for who she was and is. She rose up from that hour of prayer to face a bright new day. She felt there *was* a tomorrow for her after all. Hope came back into her heart. A few months afterwards, she was released from prison.

Unfortunately, our penal system does not always prepare people for life outside. She had no home and no one wanted to know her now. Her friends had all disappeared. She wandered along the streets crying and praying to her new-found Lord and Saviour. 'Will God really help me? Can God really deliver me?' Lost in her thoughts, right there on the pavement she was approached by a lady. This lady felt urged by the Holy Spirit to speak with her. The end result was that she found a friend and a home. God heard her prayer and delivered her from her situation. She is now reconstructing her life and is a joy to behold as one observes her sense of worth and dignity returning. She believes in herself again.

* * *

The Lord does work today to spring our traps, to open

up our prison doors, to bring hope to the hopeless and to be a friend to the friendless. He is not only the God of Moses and the children of Israel but he is also your God. Why not try him and prove him as this young lady did?

3

NOT FORGOTTEN!

Do you ever feel overwhelmed by circumstances to the point of despair? Perhaps you cannot get a job, or a close friend has moved away; it may be a long drawn-out illness or the failure of some crucial exams. Are you driven to the point of distraction by unreasonable people in your life – perhaps your parents or children, your employer or your next-door neighbour? Well, there is good news for you just as there was for the Hebrews in the days of Moses. It is recorded in very clear yet simple language that God did not forget them; God did not abandon them.

The slaves in Egypt, living under such diabolical cruelty, must often have felt forgotten. Having to endure harsh pressures for such a long period of time, they must have felt abused and broken not only physically but emotionally and spiritually. They reached wits' end corner, and there was nowhere else for them to go.

Yet it was their extremity that provided God with the opportunity to intervene and to work on their behalf. God did not forget that he had made a covenant with them. He remembered his promises to them. His eyes were on them, just as they were on the sparrow and the lillies of the field. (Matthew 6:31–34). Four hundred years before, the Lord had promised Abraham that the enslavement and oppression of his descendants would last no longer than four hundred years. And he was right on cue!

GOD HAS A PLAN

God, who must have been outraged by the inhumanity, injustice and ingratitude of the Egyptian rulers, conceived in his love a plan for his people's deliverance. While the privileged enjoyed their abuse of power, ignored the cry of the poor and exploited the underclass and powerless, God was preparing a man to lead these people out of their bondage and misery and, at the same time, was planning to execute judgement on their oppressors:

> 'Now a man of the house of Levi married a Levite woman and she became pregnant and gave birth to a son. When she saw that he was a fine child, she hid him for three months. But when she could hide him no longer, she got a papyrus basket for him and coated it with tar and pitch. Then she placed the child in it and put it among the reeds along the bank of the Nile. His sister stood at a distance to see what would happen to him.
>
> Then Pharaoh's daughter went down to the Nile

> to bathe, and her attendants were walking along the river bank. She saw the basket among the reeds and sent her slave girl to get it. She opened it and saw the baby. He was crying, and she felt sorry for him. "This is one of the Hebrew babies," she said.
>
> Then his sister asked Pharaoh's daughter, "Shall I go and get one of the Hebrew women to nurse the baby for you?"
>
> "Yes, go," she answered. And the girl went and got the baby's mother. Pharaoh's daughter said to her, "Take this baby and nurse him for me, and I will pay you." So the woman took the baby and nursed him. When the child grew older, she took him to Pharaoh's daughter and he became her son. She named him Moses, saying, "I drew him out of the water." ' *Exodus 2:1–10*

Though he was silent and seemed far away, God *was* working on his people's behalf. His silence was perplexing to say the least, yet in hindsight we now know that God was very concerned for his people. God always had a master plan to rescue and save his own. He is not taken by surprise when things 'go wrong' in our lives. He is not threatened by the people who make life difficult for us, nor is he overwhelmed by the apparent impossibilities. God's plans for us are never afterthoughts, something put together as a panic reaction. We are always God's top priority. He does not always act as quickly as we would like him to, but in his own time, when he is ready, he turns up. Who can prevent, resist or withstand him then?

If it were possible to be transported back four thousand years in time, dropped in the middle of the slave camps and brick-making mud fields, and if it were possible to mingle with those slaves, I wonder what we would hear them say. Things like, 'It would have been better if I hadn't been born.' 'Why am I here at all?' 'This isn't fair.' 'Is there a God in Heaven?' 'Even if he does exist, he obviously doesn't care about me.' The more devout among them probably prayed between sighs, 'Oh, God of our fathers, help! God of Abraham, who always keeps covenant, come down and deliver us. Remember your promise, O Lord.'

We might also discover that the more cynical and sceptical among them were growing very weary of waiting for help. They probably formed alliances with their oppressors, collaborating with them to further oppress their own people in the hope of gaining certain favours.

Others probably tried to sort things out on their own, acting in the way they thought obvious to put the situation right, not reckoning that God's way might be very different.

Moses, having grown up, was concerned for his people, and perplexed that God wasn't doing anything about them. So he decided to take things into his own hands, making use of the influential position God had given him. But, far from securing the release of his people, Moses found himself driven far away from them:

> 'One day, after Moses had grown up, he went out to where his own people were and watched them at their hard labour. He saw an Egyptian beating a Hebrew, one of his own people. Glancing this way and that and seeing no one, he killed the Egyptian and hid him in the sand. The next day he went out and saw two Hebrews fighting. He asked the one in

the wrong, "Why are you hitting your fellow Hebrew?"

The man said, "Who made you ruler and judge over us? Are you thinking of killing me as you killed the Egyptian?" Then Moses was afraid and thought, "What I did must have become known."

When Pharaoh heard of this, he tried to kill Moses, but Moses fled from Pharaoh and went to live in Midian . . .

Now a priest of Midian had seven daughters . . .

Moses agreed to stay with the man, who gave his daughter Zipporah to Moses in marriage. Zipporah gave birth to a son, and Moses named him Gershom [*Gershom* sounds like the Hebrew for *an alien there*], saying "I have become an alien in a foreign land." '

Exodus 2: 11–16, 21–22

GOD'S WAY AND GOD'S TIME

The birth and preparation of Moses to be the deliverer of God's people was one long series of miracles. It all happened in the most unlikely of ways. The unfolding drama of deliverance from Pharaoh's power is an exciting adventure but also a revelation of God's heart of love for all humanity. He who loves and cares will spare no effort to redeem his own creation from the distress and bondage that is placed on them. He will turn every stone to bring them into his peace and joy. God is *for* you not against you, just as he was for Israel, so far away and so long ago. He has not changed; his love is the same, his power is the same, his heart for you is the same.

> 'During that long period, the king of Egypt died. The Israelites groaned in their slavery and cried out, and their cry for help because of their slavery went up to God. God heard their groaning and he remembered his covenant with Abraham, with Isaac and with Jacob. So God looked on the Israelites and was concerned about them.
>
> Now Moses was tending the flock of Jethro his father-in-law, the priest of Midian, and he led the flock to the far side of the desert and came to Horeb, the mountain of God. There the angel of the Lord appeared to him in flames of fire from within a bush . . .
>
> The Lord said, "I have indeed seen the misery of my people in Egypt. I have heard them crying out because of their slave drivers, and I am concerned about their suffering. So I have come down to rescue them from the hand of the Egyptians and to bring them up out of that land into a good and spacious land, a land flowing with milk and honey . . . The cry of the Israelites has reached me, and I have seen the way the Egyptians are oppressing them. So now, go. I am sending you to Pharaoh to bring my people the Israelites out of Egypt." '
>
> *Exodus 2: 23–3:2, 7–10*

Moses was a disgraced prince and a mere shepherd, with no army, no political authority, no resources, armed only with God's word and a shepherd's rod. Yet God was telling him to go against all the terrifying might of Pharaoh, demanding, 'let my people go.' God's ways and wisdom are far higher than man's. No one in their right mind would choose to challenge the greatest political power and military might of the day. The instructions God gave Moses seemed sheer madness.

Moses must have feared that God's plan would look so ridiculous in the eyes of the Hebrews, let alone Pharaoh's. Paul, in contrast, explained to the Christians in Corinth that 'The foolishness of God is wiser than man's wisdom and the weakness of God is stronger than man's strength' (1 Corinthians 1: 25).

* * *

We are sometimes too wise and clever for our own good, relying too much on ourselves rather than trusting God's wisdom. Macken was a dapper, quick witted, genial fellow. He was always full of fun and energy. He had a marvellous conversion and a subsequent dramatic encounter with the Lord while working on the factory floor. Above all the din and clatter of machinery and activity he heard and responded to a clear commission from the Lord to be an evangelist. So he launched out in faith and soon became known for his daring faith and eloquent and anointed preaching.

He was very successful. He won many souls, planted churches, conducted missions and tent meetings. But after a few years his attention wandered and he got involved in some business ventures. At first he was well meaning; he wanted to provide finance for his evangelistic work and to supplement his income for his family. But it became obvious to his close colleagues and friends that he was losing his sense of direction and was being diverted from his vision and calling.

He was counselled and warned to change and return to his original vision. Sadly he ignored the warnings, even laughed them off. He thought he was always a few steps ahead of his rather 'slow' contemporaries. He was so sure of himself, so confident in his own abilities.

Soon he became involved with other women. Eventually he became bankrupt, his marriage broke up and it remains a casualty to this day. He was a sad loss for us all, especially his lovely family. If only he had listened to God's alternative way!

* * *

What appears as the foolishness and weakness of God's way is far more dynamic than all the cleverness and power of men put together. There is a dynamism in the presence of God which surpasses all else. That power is released into our situation when we believe and obey God.

CALLED TO BE FREE

'I have indeed seen the misery of my people in Egypt,' the Lord said (Exodus 3:7). God saw and felt their deep sorrows and inner pain; and he heard their cry for deliverance, freedom and healing. They cried and he came! In his coming the impossible happened: he invited them to go free, to be healed. He offered them his abundance and fulness, and promised them 'a land flowing with milk and honey' – figurative language, emphasising prosperity, success and abundance.

To be able to enjoy God we need to be free. Freedom is in vogue. We live in an age that cries out for freedom and, in recent times, have witnessed with great delight the joy with which people who were bound by political systems and ideologies have come into freedom. The cry for freedom rings deep in the heart of each of us. We want to be free to pursue our own goals and ambitions in life, free to follow the convictions of our own hearts, free to live where we want to, to eat what we want to, to choose our religious and political persuasions. In short, we want to be free from the dictates and domination of others, whether through personal and direct means or by the more sinister and subtle ways of systems and structures which rob us of the right to follow our own heart.

Anyone or anything which robs us of our human value and dignity must be regarded as an oppressor. We cannot really reach God's ultimate for us until we are *free* to be all that God intended us to be. God has a plan for each of us, a future in which we can develop our potential to the fullest, that we might mirror his own beauty to the world.

So God calls us to be free, free from the many bondages that the enemy places on us. We need to be free to be ourselves, not always striving to live up to the expectations of others. Free from the pressures and anxieties of everyday life, its tensions and worry. Free from the sense of guilt, the penalty and the pollution of sin. Paul said, 'We are no longer slaves to sin and sin should no longer have dominion over us' (Romans 6:7, NASB). To be really free we must hang our hang-ups and crucify our idiosyncracies, becoming instead 'slaves to righteousness' (Romans 6:18).

True freedom is not 'being independent'. It is knowing that God has touched our lives by his grace and liberated us from all our fears and our inhibitions, in order for us to be unique, free to be secure in ourselves and in God's love. Insecurity is a tormenting thing but when God sets us free we can rest in the certainty that he is on our side. We can be conquerors in all things.

We do not need to come under pressure to conform to others. True freedom is that liberty from within that enables us to stand in our own right and be the people God intended us to be.

In order for God to bring the people of Israel into all that he promised them, he had first to free them from the domination of Pharaoh and the environment of Egypt. To bring them *into* what he promised, he had to bring them *out*. There is a parallel here for us. If we are to come into all the blessings, riches and fulness of God we must first be willing for God to free us from the things that belong to sin, the devil and the world dominated by Satan – its pleasures, principles, spirits, system. We cannot enjoy God's fulness if we are not willing to be freed from the chains of the past.

Unfortunately, many people want to enjoy the best of both worlds, to sit on the fence as it were, to have one foot in each camp. This cannot be. Jesus himself said that we cannot serve God and mammon; we either come under the Lordship of Christ or the tyranny of the devil. Just as God raised up Moses to be the deliverer for the people of Israel, he sent Jesus to be our deliverer. He is well aware that we can never free ourselves by our own strength, schemes, righteousness or goodness, from the strong chains of pride, lust, greed and selfishness that bind us. Only God can do this.

Real freedom is not freedom to do as we please but freedom to do as God pleases. It lies in knowing God and his ways. Real freedom is to live in accordance with God's will for us, living within the limits and boundaries set for us by God. This makes good sense: he who created us knows us best. He knows our tolerance and stress levels, our responses and defence mechanisms. He understands what the consequences for us will be if we allow alien elements into our makeup: it will foul up our systems! Real liberty is not licence to do as we please; it is the liberty to make the right kind of choices in life and to accept responsibility for our decisions and actions. God knows that the devil's intention is to destroy us and if we step into the devil's territory we are liable to be devoured. That is why God has put up some perimeters for us and if we keep within those perimeters we are safe, protected from the enemy.

True liberty behaves in a manner that is consistent with God's higher purposes for us. We are created in God's image, so a person who is really free has the ability to respect others and to live within the bounds of decency, has a conscience free of guilt and condemnation, and has the strength to say no to things she knows are wrong and detrimental to her welfare. Freedom is the inner strength to follow your own convictions, not to yield to the pressures of society or your peers just to keep up with the 'in crowd', even if it means that you stand out and look odd.

Moses' parents, and later Moses himself, demonstrated this quality when they were willing to stand up to Pharaoh and go against his decrees. They dared to be different because they believed in God's higher calling and purposes for them.

To live in God's perfect will, and do it in God's ordained way, is the best guarantee for fulfilment and satisfaction. To settle for less is to live below our real potential. Not only do we jeopardise the only sure basis for our development, but we leave ourselves vulnerable to being drawn back into a tangled web of bondage.

BECOMING FREE

The freedom God offers us, like the freedom he offered the Hebrews, does not come automatically or by wishful thinking. We need to press on towards it with determination. Paul said, 'Forgetting what is behind and straining towards what is ahead, I press on towards the goal to win the prize for which God has called me heavenwards in Christ Jesus' (Philippians 3:13–14).

So what steps can we take to help ourselves move into the freedom God offers us? We can take some clues from the reaction of the elders of the people when Moses, and his brother Aaron, told them what God was proposing to do:

> 'Moses and Aaron brought together all the elders of the Israelites, and Aaron told them everything the Lord had said to Moses. He also performed the signs before the people, and they believed. And when they heard that the Lord was concerned about them and had seen their misery, they bowed down and worshipped.' *Exodus 4:29–31*

Realise that God is on your side

God is offering you a solution, a way out, a miracle! So don't just sit there and carry on as usual. Where would Moses and his people be now if they had adopted a negative, disbelieving attitude? Still in Egypt.

Decide to worship God

This doesn't always come easily! But it is the logical follow-on from realising that God is on your side. An open attitude of faith in what God has promised, no matter how unlikely it seems, will lead us to worship him. On the other hand, if we are too wary of being 'caught out', not at all sure that we have really heard God properly, we may become cynical and sceptical. It is important to check out, with mature Christian friends, what we think God is telling us. The elders that Moses spoke to must have spent some time discussing what he said, trying to decide whether this promise of freedom was in line with what they knew of God's character and earlier promises. But once they were sure, they made up their minds to believe him and to worship him.

Cooperate with God

When the prodigal son 'came to his senses' in that far away country, and realised there was hope for him if he went back to his father, he didn't just carry on sitting there hoping something would happen. He did something about it. He got up, shook the dust off his rags and started walking the long road back home (Luke 15). In the same way, the Hebrew elders did not resign themselves to 'fate'. When they chose, in faith, to believe that God was telling them to move on, they decided to cooperate with him. So they took the first steps on a very long journey with him which would eventually lead them to freedom and fulfilment.

In our own experiences of being delivered from the chains which bind us, and being gently nudged by God to take steps into the freedom he longs to give us, we will have problems and face seemingly insurmountable odds. But with God on our side, worship in our hearts and a willingness to cooperate with him in the journey, the future is assured.

* * *

John and Jane are such lovely people. They met while studying and fell in love. Both qualified and were established in their respective careers. They had a lovely church wedding surrounded by their friends; then came home-building and having children. They had quite a financial struggle in the early years but they were both successful in their respective fields. The children grew and life prospered. But just as they began to enjoy the fruits of their hard work over the years, John started to fool around, first with one woman, then another. His unfaithfulness was followed by abuse and public humiliation. Jane held on, hoping to save the marriage, and holding it together for the sake of their four children. The stress and uncertainty began to sap her health and hope. She couldn't sleep at nights, she lost her smile, her sadness could be seen and felt. She was at breaking point, her profile bent, her heart broken. Then, one day she met Jesus who gave her new hope and new life. She was able to forgive her husband and those who wronged her. He, however, left the home but she has her smile back. She has picked up the pieces of her life again. You wouldn't believe it was the same person! She learnt how to forgive, how to break the hold that bitterness could have, and move on to enjoy the freedom Jesus gives.

4

BROUGHT OUT TO BRING INTO

God is not a spoil-sport. He is not a killjoy. God does not withhold anything good from anyone. Instead, he specialises in removing misery from people's lives. Many people believe that to serve God is to lose out on life. To be a Christian is to become some sort of religious nut or fanatic. Their image of a Christian is of someone who misses all the fun and adventure in life. Nothing could be further from the truth! The Bible's picture of people who served God reflects people whose lives are full of substance, meaning and purpose. They were ordinary people who experienced extraordinariness once God came into their lives. They were people who were prepared to sacrifice much and suffer hardship to preserve the priceless treasure which they found in God. Their fun, pleasure and adventure were derived from the satisfaction that they were doing God's will and living God's way.

'I have promised to bring you up out of your misery

in Egypt into . . . a land flowing with milk and honey,' was what God said to Moses (Exodus 3:17). God came down to deliver, to bring out and to bring into. Not just to bring them out of bondage and Egypt, but also to lead them into a place of promise. He had a long-term purpose for them: he wanted them to be whole, fulfilled.

> ' "Go, assemble the elders of Israel and say to them, 'The Lord, the God of your fathers, the God of Abraham, Isaac and Jacob, appeared to me and said: I have watched over you and have seen what has been done to you in Egypt. And I have promised to bring you up out of your misery in Egypt into the land of the Canaanites, Hittites, Amorites, Perizzites, Hivites and Jebusites – a land flowing with milk and honey.'
>
> The elders of Israel will listen to you. Then you and the elders are to go to the king of Egypt and say to him, 'The Lord, the God of the Hebrews, has met with us. Let us take a three-day journey into the desert to offer sacrifices to the Lord our God.' But I know that the king of Egypt will not let you go unless a mighty hand compels him. So I will stretch out my hand and strike the Egyptians with all the wonders that I will perform among them. After that, he will let you go.
>
> And I will make the Egyptians favourably disposed towards his people, so that when you leave you will not go empty-handed. Every woman is to ask her neighbour and any woman living in her house for articles of silver and gold and for clothing, which you will put on your sons and daughters. And so you will plunder the Egyptians." ' *Exodus 3:16–22*

Some churches and Christians present an unhelpful picture of the Christian life. For some reason they think that to be a child of God they have to be austere, adopt an ascetic lifestyle, be cut off from reality, suppress natural urges to enjoy themselves, and be controlled by some kind of regimented system. They are people who look as though they were baptised in lime juice. They wear sad, long, donkey faces, and believe that you cannot enjoy life, have fun, enjoy music and pleasure and be happy with your friends as a Christian. These stereotypes may date back to the middle ages but they are not found in the Bible. They totally misrepresent the Christian life and have nothing to do with the biblical idea of being a child of God.

Jesus said, 'I have come that they may have life, and have it to the full' (John 10:10). Contrary to popular opinion, Jesus doesn't call us into a vacuum, he calls us to fulness. His purpose is to fill our lives with peace, joy and love, to give us back our self-esteem, self-worth and dignity. He doesn't call us to aimlessness and emptiness but to a meaningful and purposeful life, a life of content and quality. Life with Jesus is an exciting exploration of life in all its vicissitudes. It is as God intended, an exploration which will last for ever.

God brought Israel out of Egypt to bring them into the Land of Promise. He brings us out of a life that is going nowhere, out of bondage, deprivation, suffering and emptiness and brings us into a life that is going places. He brings us out of an existence that has nothing of real, lasting value to bring us into something with eternal value.

CALLED FOR A PURPOSE

Some people feel very comfortable with 'religiosity'. But Jesus didn't die to bring us into religiosity but into reality. Many Christians have been brought out but have not yet been brought into an experience of the abundant provision God has made for them. Many have got stuck, others have stagnated. They are those who live out a lie, they have a form of godliness but they deny the power that genuine godliness would bring. They do not know the dynamism and vibrancy of Christ's life within them. They are so religious they have forgotten how to be real.

Many people live behind a mask pretending to be what they are not. Some Christians have a mask that they wear on Sundays, another mask when they meet their neighbours, another when the pastor is visiting or when their friends come around. The real self is the one hardly seen by others; the smiling face hides a bleeding heart. Some people, when you ask them how they are, will say, 'I am fine!' when deep down inside they are hurting, frustrated, tense, under stress. Yet they keep up an endless charade because they fear that if people knew what they were really like they would be rejected. Such fears lead to religiosity rather than reality. A Christian must first accept the truth about himself or herself. When we are honest enough to face up to reality and stop pretending, then Jesus can begin to bring us out of our needs, problems, pressures and heartaches and bring us into his own goodness, grace, power and provision. Jesus died to bring us out of all that tortures and torments us, and into his love and grace.

In the historic encounter Moses had with the Lord at

the burning bush, the Lord sent him to confront Pharaoh with the demand, 'let my people go'. But at the same time God commissioned Moses to bring his people into a land 'flowing with milk and honey'. God had no intention whatever of leaving the people he delivered in no-man's land. The redeemed of the Lord do not exist in limbo. God clearly calls us out of the spirit and systems of the world, from the things that oppress and depress us. But he does not leave us there to wander aimlessly. He calls us into the rich inheritance of God's very own children, which he has prepared for us in Christ.

In practice, this means two things:

- *We are free to enjoy life!* Some Christians get so super-spiritual they cannot relate to the ordinary, everyday things of life. They cannot enjoy creation and the things that God has given because they have a false idea of spirituality and true holiness. We are called to enjoy all the creativity, zest, life and power of God himself.
- *God has a definite purpose for each of us.* It is a purpose conceived in love, specifically designed to suit each individual, tailored to each person's uniqueness, abilities and gifts. The Lord declares, 'I know the plans that I have for you . . . plans to prosper you and not to harm you, plans to give you hope and a future' (Jeremiah 29:11). The Lord has a plan specifically tailored to suit you and no one else can fit into that plan except you. God has your best interest at heart. Unfortunately, though many people believe this, they never stop to find out what God's plan is for their lives. To do so, we need to take time to seek the Lord. Ask him

concerning his will and his plan for your life. He brought you out of your waywardness and 'ownwayness' in order to bring you into the centre of his will and way. And he has promised, 'Call upon me and come and pray to me, and I will listen to you. You will seek me and find me when you seek me with all your heart. I will be found by you' (Jeremiah 29:12–14).

CALLED TO BE WHOLE

We are called to be whole as much as we are called to be free. God will have it no other way. He reminded his people, through Moses, that he was the origin of their existence and the fulfilment of all their needs, when he said 'I am who I am.'

> 'But Moses said to God, "Who am I, that I should go to Pharaoh and bring the Israelites out of Egypt?"
>
> And God said, "I will be with you. And this will be the sign to you that it is I who have sent you: When you have brought the people out of Egypt, you will worship God on this mountain."
>
> Moses said to God, "Suppose I go to the Israelites and say to them, 'The God of your fathers has sent me to you,' and they ask me, 'What is his name?' Then what shall I tell them?"
>
> God said to Moses, "I am who I am. This is what you are to say to the Israelites: I AM has sent me to you." ' *Exodus 3:11–14*

God revealed himself as the all-sufficient one. He invites us to draw from his all sufficiency to fill our need. His desire and purpose for us flow out of the depth of his own eternal being and character.

All God's dealings with people are rooted in who he is as a person. 'I am who I am' or 'I will be what I will be', the Lord said to Moses, 'so that you can be all that you were meant to be.' God's will for us is rooted deep in the very nature of who he is. God lacks nothing, he is not deficient in any way. He is the only being who is not dependent on anything or anyone else for his existence. He is both self-existent and all-sufficient; he is complete. It is to this completeness that God now calls us. When he said to Moses, 'Go and tell them I am sending you,' he gave an open invitation to share his life so that we too will lack nothing, and be free from our own deficiencies which demoralise and defeat us.

Whenever God gives a revelation of himself it is never just for the sake of it. God is not in the business of amusing or entertaining people nor is he in the business of proving a point. He is not in the business of showing off. These disclosures of himself are always meant to be means by which he communicates his character to us that we may know him, and by knowing him come to trust his love, know his will and experience his power to care for his own. God was saying to Moses, ' "I AM" is not just a past, abstract existence but a present active person. I will cause things to happen! Because of what I am about to do in you and these people, all the world through succeeding generations will know that I am the real, true and living God.'

Shalom

This offer to enjoy total well-being is very exciting. The

theme runs right through the Bible. It is an important concept, mentioned no less than 237 times in the Old Testament. It is also a New Testament concept. The angel announced to Mary and Joseph that they should call their baby Jesus, 'for he shall save people from their sins' (Matthew 1:25). The word for 'save' is a Greek equivalent of the Hebrew word for 'wholeness' in the Old Testament. The Hebrew word is *shalom*, the New Testament *sozo*, which means salvation. Jesus saves totally. A whole salvation for the whole person.

It was common practice in Old Testament times to exchange greetings. When you met your family, relatives, friends, neighbours, even strangers, you would say '*shalom*', much the same as we today would say, 'good morning, how are you?' *Shalom* means: peace, welfare, health, completeness. It was meant to be a sincere enquiry into the well being of the person. 'How is your peace?' 'Are you prospering and in good health?' 'Are you enjoying inner harmony with yourself?' 'Are you enjoying harmony with your neighbours?' It is this wholeness, completeness, total well-being that God intends for us, just as he did for his people in Egypt. That is why God, in his love for us, sent his Son to atone for our sins, to pay the full price necessary for our redemption, to destroy all the works of the devil and to make it possible for us to break free from all the chains that bind us. He offers us new life. It's full, free and well worth it! *Shalom, sozo.* Hallelujah!

STEPS TO WHOLENESS

What steps can we take in order to become the whole

people God intended us to be?

1 Be real with God

Come to a realisation of your own condition and need. Do not kid yourself. Do not pretend. Do not hide behind a mask of unreality, even if it is religious! It is time to face up to yourself and to confront your problems. Do not make excuses for your failure or seek to justify or defend yourself; it is much better to accept responsibility for your own decisions and choices. Recognise sin where there is sin. Do not dress it up or seek to rename it. God knows what we are really like. To make yourself vulnerable to God is not weakness. Drop your guards and defences. Maybe it's rather embarrassing to accept that your dreams lie shattered at your feet – but how liberating it is when we can accept the truth and not seek to escape it!

2 Trust God's love for you

Have faith in God's love and ability to redeem you from whatever your condition or need. It is important that you trust in God's great big heart for you. He does really care. Whatever your guilt he still loves you and wants to deliver you. Faith is the only means by which we can appropriate the blessings of God in our life. It is the ability to believe that God means what he says and that he is able to do what he says. It is a deliberate act whereby we choose to accept as fact what God says rather than depend on our feelings. Our feelings can be misleading and unstable to say the least! We are subject to moods and changes, but God never changes. What

God says is exactly what he means. If he says that he cares for you then he does care. Faith is that quiet inner conviction that God does not lie.

There's another reason why we need to trust ourselves to God. Our assessment of our situation could be very wrong. We do not know everything about ourselves; we are not aware of all the things that have made us who we are. God is fully aware, in possession of all the facts. And he will work in us to spring the traps we are in, one by one – traps we might still be only dimly aware of. Paul, when encouraging the Christians in Ephesus, said that God 'is able to do immeasurably more than all we ask or imagine, according to his power that is at work within us' (Ephesians 3:20).

So we cannot say yet exactly *what* God will do when we begin to trust him, but we can be sure it will be nothing but the best!

Faith is not an anti-intellectual exercise nor sentimental subjectivism. It means, rather, having the honesty to face reality, the courage to admit our own limitations, and the good sense to invite God to intervene in our affairs.

3 Accept God's forgiveness

To be whole it is crucial to know that you are forgiven, that God has cleansed you from all your sins and washed away all your guilt, that your past is buried in the sea of God's forgetfulness. The apostle John says, 'If we confess our sins, God is faithful and just and will forgive us our sins and purify us from all unrighteousness' (1 John 1:9). We need to have that deep assurance that we are justified by faith in Jesus, 'justified' meaning that we now stand forgiven before God as though we have never sinned. How? Because Jesus died on the cross to bring us grace. We cannot obtain God's forgiveness by our own good works. Never. We are only forgiven and justified in the eyes of God by our faith in the merits of Jesus' sacrifice. When he died on the cross he made a complete offering so that we no longer need to be afraid. So we can come boldly to God and find forgiveness. 'If anyone is in Christ, he is a new creation; the old has gone, the new has come! (2 Corinthians 5:17). The old life with all its sin, its uncleanness and all its unpleasant past is forgiven, not because God is soft but because he is gracious. 'For we are saved by grace not by works, so that no man would be able to boast in the face of God' (Ephesians 2:8–190, NASB). We need to know that 'there is now no condemnation for those who are in Christ Jesus' (Romans 8:1).

Jesus died in your place to give you forgiveness. Accept it. Don't punish yourself any longer. He has forgiven you: now forgive yourself.

4 Learn how to forgive others

You also need to learn how to forgive others who have hurt you.

Jesus tells the story of a man who had a large debt to pay. He went to his master to ask for longer to pay it, but the master completely forgave him and cancelled his debt. He was released! On his way home he met a man who owed him a few pennies. Instead of showing mercy as he had received mercy he demanded every last penny. He treated his fellow man very badly. He could not forgive the other man his debt as he had been forgiven of his. His master, hearing what he had done, called him back and made him pay the full penalty (Matthew 18:21–35). It is a very precious experience to know the love of God in your heart to such an extent that you are able to forgive those who have wronged you, those who have taken advantage over you, abused and hurt you. It is a releasing experience. To be unforgiving in spirit is to open the door to bitterness and sourness. It is creating holes in your life through which the blessings, peace and joy of God will leak away. We need to forgive others and accept them exactly as Christ has forgiven us and accepted us (see Romans 15:7).

It is not easy to forgive people. Sometimes we feel a lot more comfortable with the hurt and grief because we feel wronged. We feed our wounds when we refuse to forgive others. But this will damage and stunt us spiritually. We need to know forgiveness for ourselves and also be willing and ready to forgive others who have sinned against us.

5 Relate to God as your Father

We need to live under the constant knowledge of God's Fatherhood. We need to understand that God is not only God of all creation but he is also our Father. Many people have great difficulty in relating to God as Father because they had unpleasant experiences in their own childhood. They may have had unhelpful role models of fatherhood. They may have even been rejected, dominated or abused by their father.

Some people don't even know who their father is. Because of this lack in their lives they find it very difficult to relate to God as Father. But God longs for us to have a relationship with him that is intimate and loving. He wants to love us as his children. That is why Jesus taught his disciples to pray, 'our Father', not just, 'O Almighty God.' No. Our God, our Father.

Paul told the Roman Christians that those 'who are led by the Spirit of God are sons of God. For you did not receive a spirit that makes you a slave again to fear, but you received the spirit of sonship. And by him we cry, "*Abba*, Father." The Spirit himself testifies with our spirit that we are God's children' (Romans 8:14–16). Not outcasts, but children of God. God made a covenant with his people. He said, 'I will live with them and walk among them, and I will be their God, and they will be my people . . . I will be a Father to you and you will be my sons and daughters, says the Lord Almighty' (2 Corinthians 6:16,18). The Lord invites us into a father/child relationship with himself.

The fatherhood of God goes far beyond anything that human fatherhood could represent. He loves without partiality. He cares for us even when we may not be very deserving. He deals with us in love and kindness. He never forgets, forsakes or turns his back on us. To be whole we need to receive acceptance, approval and affirmation from our Father. We need to enjoy his constant love, protection, and provision.

All God's children should have one burning passion in their hearts: to please their Father. Only when this is our over-riding aim will we be able to resist the temptations to go our own way, doing what we feel we want to rather than what is right. But we need have no fear of reprisals from God. He *will* discipline us, as a good father does, but he does so gently and in love.

We may need to reprogramme our understanding of fatherhood. Some only know fathers who dominate; they now need to reset their minds to relate to God as a Father who wants the best for them. Some people only know a father who is selfish and tyrannical; they need to learn to recognise that God loves and cares like a mother, as a shepherd cares for hand-reared lambs. Some people only know a father who is demanding; here is a Father who is giving. Some people only know a father who is weak; here is a Father who is strong yet gentle and loving. To be whole we need to know and enjoy the fatherhood of God.

6 Share God's wholeness with others

To be whole we need to enjoy friendship with Jesus. That's mind-blowing! Jesus is God! Yet we are called not to be his servants but his friends (see John 15:14–15). He invites us into an intimate fellowship with God and with one another. Wholeness will not come unless we are really sharing our new life in Christ with each other. In the New Testament this special quality and depth of friendship that Christians share with each other is called *koinonia*. It means fellowship that is genuinely based on love, trust, loyalty and deep commitment to one another.

The New Testament makes it clear that one of the secrets of the early church's success, dynamism and impact on society was their *koinonia* friendship with each other. They were a community who loved deeply and showed the love of God in practical ways. They even sold their possessions in order to give to those who had nothing (Acts 2:42–47). We need to return to this kind of unselfish love and practice if we would enjoy God's fulness and wholeness.

God wants us to enjoy the good things of earth. The only thing that is taboo with God is sin and uncleanness. We have every right to enjoy the things God has created, we even have a right to possess them, providing we are good stewards of them. When we put the good things of God to wrong uses, then they become a problem. When things in our lives become more significant to us than God is, they become our idols and keep us from whole-hearted devotion to God. We become self indulgent and neglect the needs of others, when what God requires of us is to steward properly and profitably the things which he has given us so freely to enjoy. It is part of God's love towards us to hold us accountable to him for all that he has placed in our hands.

To be whole means to know deliverance and discipline, freedom and forgiveness, fellowship and stewardship, enjoyment of God and service of one another, abundance and accountability.

5

MOVING ON

'When Pharaoh let the people go, God did not lead them on the road through the Philistine country, though that was shorter. For God said, "If they face war, they might change their minds and return to Egypt." So God led the people around by the desert road towards the Red Sea. The Israelites went up out of Egypt armed for battle.

Moses took the bones of Joseph with him because Joseph had made the sons of Israel swear an oath. He had said, "God will surely come to your aid, and then you must carry my bones up with you from this place."

After leaving Succoth they camped at Etham on the edge of the desert. By day the Lord went ahead of them in a pillar of cloud to guide them on their way and by night in a pillar of fire to give them light, so that they could travel by day or night. Neither the pillar of cloud by day nor the pillar of fire by night left its place in front of the people.'

Exodus 13:17–22

The Lord calls us to follow where he leads. Through all their journeys the people of Israel followed the cloud by day and pillar of fire by night. The two were symbols of the presence of the Lord. Every disciple of Christ is called to a personal pilgrimage with God. Indeed the highest accolade that could be given to any mortal is that he is called to walk with God.

A PERSONAL PILGRIMAGE

God called Abraham to leave his people and to step out into the unknown. In obedience he followed and so altered the course of history. He became a partner with God in fulfilment of the plan of redemption: 'all peoples on earth will be blessed through you,' God told him (Genesis 12:3).

One of the most outstanding men of the Old Testament was Enoch: 'Enoch walked with God; then he was no more, because God took him away' (Genesis 5:24). His fellowship with God was so intimate and consistent that he simply carried on walking with him and apparently by-passed death (see Hebrews 11:5).

To be a pilgrim with God is the experience of a lifetime and should not be missed for all the tea in China or all the gold in India! To walk with God is very exciting, yet exacting. It is a life full of suspense and adventure and yet none of it is 'make believe'.

It is a personalised affair between God and you. No two people are called to the same journey. There may be certain similarities but God has carefully planned a path for each individual. My wife and I are blessed with identical twin daughters. They are so alike that although they are now in their twenties I still mix them up! Yet I can tell them apart by their laughter, the way they reason things out, their priorities and their different personalities. Twins but not clones. Just as God has made each of us with our own uniqueness, so he has a plan and pathway specially tailored for each of us.

The Christian life is the progressive life. A life of movement, going forward, constant steady growth. There is no room for stagnation. In the story of the children of Israel such phrases like, 'they set out', 'journeyed', 'sojourned', 'went out', 'Moses led them out', appear with almost monotonous regularity. They were always kept on the move even when it was not always comfortable or convenient. They moved from one experience to another. They probably did not realise that they had embarked on a journey which would have such serious implications. The road to the Promised Land was full of the unexpected. Had they known all that was involved and the events that awaited them, they may not have been so willing to follow Moses. Their experiences on the way included the marvellous and the miraculous. They ranged from rejoicing to mourning, from triumph to trials, from celebrations to complaining, from the mountain tops to darkest valleys, from mighty deliverances to disgraceful defeats, from the sublime to the ridiculous. And God never failed them. Years afterwards, the prophet Jeremiah exclaimed:

> 'The steadfast love of the Lord never ceases,
>   his mercies never come to an end;
> they are new every morning;
>   great is thy faithfulness.'
>
> *Lamentations 3:22–23, RSV*

The success or failure of the Israelites on their journey depended solely on their ability to trust God and obey him implicitly, in every circumstance. When they did this they were utterly blessed and prospered. When they rebelled and disobeyed they met with disaster.

ON THE MOVE

To be a pilgrim is to be a pioneer not a settler, one who passes through life as if in search of a higher goal, one who is a stranger, an alien searching for a better country (see Hebrews 11:16). Part and parcel of our walk with God, as with any pioneering, are difficulties and problems. We will be called to endure times of testing and trial, as the children of Israel did. But the exciting thing is to see how God enables us to cope in the different situations which are far beyond our own capacity to manage. Each trial provides an opportunity to release our faith, to tap into the unlimited resources of God and to see how God intervenes to change the natural course of things. As the writer to the New Testament Hebrews put it: 'We taste the goodness of the word of God and the powers of the coming age' (Hebrews 6:5). Each difficulty gives us a chance to see the power of God released into the practicalities of everyday life. A Christian should be 'supernaturally natural and naturally supernatural', that is, by faith we bring God into our everyday life. Christianity is immensely practical. It is not just theory or religious jargon but it has to do with real life. It is down to earth but not earthbound. It is sufficiently heavenly minded to do a whole lot of earthly good.

A vision for the future

To be a pilgrim is to learn how to triumph against incredible odds and impossible situations by the help of the Holy Spirit. Paul puts it this way: 'If God is for us, who can be against us?' 'In all these things we are more than conquerors.' 'I can do everything through him who gives me strength.' 'And my God will meet all your needs according to his glorious riches in Christ Jesus.' (See Romans 8:31, 37; Philippians 4:13, 19.) To be a pilgrim with Jesus is to dream dreams when others are filled with hopelessness and despair. It is to be captivated by a vision of the future when others can see nothing but the problems of today. Each achievement becomes a stepping stone for another. Each new experience awakens new hunger to reach greater heights. Each victory inspires us to win another victory. A pilgrim enjoys today but lives for tomorrow. He does not get buried in his yesterdays, nor does he allow the past to determine the future. His spirit is always restless to pursue God's highest and best.

A pilgrim is possessed with a passion to experience all that God has promised, accomplish all that God commands, and take every opportunity to expand his horizons. He or she always seems to be gripped with what some might think an 'unhealthy' preoccupation with things that are 'higher', 'weightier' and out of the ordinary (see Colossians 3:1–3). He has been enamoured with things which don't seem to occupy the attention of the ordinary, 'pedestrian' Christian. Things which don't appear very important in the natural course of events capture his imagination. The pilgrim is not a settler; he or she can prove to be a pain in the neck to others! She never seems satisfied with what she has accomplished or experienced. A real sense of holy dissatisfaction beats in her heart. There is always another mountain to climb, another giant to conquer, another river to cross, another village or town to be reached.

Although we must be careful to avoid a spirituality that is based on performance, we cannot but admire the person whose heart is so captivated by God and motivated to please him in all things, that he is not content to exist in passive mediocrity. Instead, he burns with 'holy aggression', always striving for the excellence worthy of his calling and befitting his King.

Pilgrims together

Deliverance from bondage in Egypt, and their newfound freedom, were not all that God had intended for his people. They still had a long way to go. Those whom God delivered must now be discipled and trained to live and work as a community and be prepared for nationhood. To turn a disorganised, quarrelsome and faithless multitude (as they proved to be) into a nation worthy of bearing the name of the Lord and being of service to others, was no mean task.

No pilgrim is meant to function as a solo performer but to find his or her place within the community of God's people and discover his or her gifting in order to make a valid contribution to the whole. We need each other. It is crucial to our progress and personal walk with God that we learn to work as part of a team (see 1 Corinthians 12:14–27). Each new phase in the Israelite's lives, every new step, was to contribute to their overall development as a community.

As it was with them so it is with us. That we too will be tested is a certainty. How we cope in our hour of testing will determine our destiny in God. Our ability to cope and come out victorious is a true indicator of our level of maturity in God. Our metal will be tried.

COPING WITH ENEMY ATTACKS

When Pharaoh learnt that the Hebrews had left Egypt and were heading for the Red Sea he gathered his forces and pursued them with the sole intention of destroying them. The Lord had specifically instructed Moses to take a longer route, though it was possible to go a much shorter way from Etham, situated on the edge of the wilderness. Pharaoh mistakenly felt that they were 'wandering aimlessly' and felt he had a good chance to overtake and overwhelm them. He spared no effort. He gathered six hundred of his best chariots, and all his horses, army and officers and gave chase. The children of Israel were camped at Pi Hahiroth, in front of the sea and wedged between two mountains. Suddenly, they looked up. Horror! Panic! The Egyptian army was marching after them!

> 'As Pharaoh approached, the Israelites looked up, and there were the Egyptians, marching after them. They were terrified and cried out to the Lord. They said to Moses, "Was it because there were no graves in Egypt that you brought us to the desert to die? What have you done to us by bringing us out of Egypt? Didn't we say to you in Egypt, 'Leave us alone; let us serve the Egyptians'? It would have

> been better for us to serve the Egyptians than to die in the desert!" ' *Exodus 14:10–12*

A pilgrim must expect counter attacks. The enemy will pursue us with a vengeance! Attacks by the enemy can either overwhelm us and put such fear in our hearts that we are driven to panic, or they drive us to the Lord. How we cope in these situations, in fear or faith, will determine success or failure.

In an instant the people had moved from glorious freedom into extreme danger. What consternation! What a dilemma! Suddenly given freedom; now just as suddenly confronted with annihilation. Pharaoh planned to destroy them. What Pharaoh did not know was that God planned to destroy Pharaoh. What the people of Israel did not realise was that God was neither surprised nor threatened by this turn of events. He was always in control.

What *was* surprising was the people's distrust and sheer ingratitude. God had brought about their release from Egypt by the most amazing series of miracles – but already they were complaining. Perhaps they thought they had had their run of luck and God had no more ideas left up his sleeve. They turned on Moses as if he was the villain, the cause of their problem. You can never win with some people! One moment a hero, a great leader, the next moment they were ready to kill him. People are so unpredictable. They do and say very strange things when under pressure.

Not much has changed with the passage of time. We too must be prepared to face blatant attacks from Satan. We will be pursued relentlessly, and in a variety of ways. Satan will employ any means to stop us from going forward. He will find ways to harass and distress us, his purpose always being to defeat us. Persecution, slander, disillusionment, division, discouragement, oppression and depression are some of his favourite tactics. Satan is no gentleman. He exploits our weak points and will kick us while we're down. He will turn against us those people from whom we least expect opposition, often those we trust most. Attacks will come directly and indirectly from within and without.

Those who are determined to follow Christ, who set their hearts to be godly, must expect this. Satan won't tamely surrender. He won't let us go without a fight. However, we do not need to fear him but to have courage and confidence, 'because the one who is in you is greater than the one who is in the world' (1 John 4:4). Be bold and strong. We know our God is able to protect and deliver us. He is not a let-down. Not a failure. Our extremity offers God a golden opportunity to prove his love, care and faithfulness towards us.

> 'Moses answered the people, "Do not be afraid. Stand firm and you will see the deliverance the Lord will bring you today. The Egyptians you see today you will never see again. The Lord will fight for you; you need only to be still." ' *Exodus 14:13–14*

In the times of our fiercest battles we must learn the secret which gave Moses such courage and fortitude in the face of impending disaster. As the Egyptian army marched on them, the people panicked but Moses looked to God. His instant reaction was not fear, but faith. Because of this he was able to comfort and encourage this frightened, distraught people, 'Do not be afraid. Stand firm and you will see the deliverance the Lord will bring you today.' It is the same for us. When our lives seem out of control – things are going wrong at work, arguments blow up from nowhere in our families, or we feel totally inadequate, a failure at everything we have turned our hands to – Moses reminds us not to let fear get the better of us. Satan will try to make us panic, to 'throw us into confusion' so that we cannot think straight and immediately begin to despair. Instead, we need only to call on God, to hand the problem over to him, to 'stand firm' and 'to be still'. 'If God is for us, who can be against us?' (Romans 8:31).

> 'Then Moses stretched out his hand over the sea, and all that night the Lord drove the sea back with a strong east wind and turned it into dry land. The waters were divided, and the Israelites went through the sea on dry ground, with a wall of water on their right and on their left.
>
> The Egyptians pursued them, and all Pharaoh's horses and chariots and horsemen followed them into the sea . . .
>
> Then the Lord said to Moses, "Stretch out your hand over the sea so that the waters may flow back over the Egyptians and their chariots and horsemen." Moses stretched out his hand over the sea, and at daybreak the sea went back to its place. The Egyptians were fleeing towards it, and the Lord swept them into the sea. The water flowed back and covered the chariots and horsemen – the entire army of Pharaoh that had followed the Israelites into the sea. Not one of them survived.'
>
> *Exodus 14:21–23, 26–28*

TIME FOR CELEBRATION

The Lord worked such a resounding victory there at the Red Sea that, even today, it stands unparalleled and unchallenged as a testimony to God's faithfulness. He is a God who will always stand up alongside his people to vindicate them and defend them. He dares anyone to mess with his people. No wonder they sang, 'The Lord will reign for ever and ever' (Exodus 15:18). There is a song and celebration dance for everyone who will not panic in impossible situations but has the good sense to trust God instead:

> 'When Pharaoh's horses, chariots and horsemen went into the sea, the Lord brought the waters of the sea back over them, but the Israelites walked through the sea on dry ground. Then Miriam the prophetess, Aaron's sister, took a tambourine in her hand, and all the women followed her, with tambourines and dancing. Miriam sang to them:
>
> "Sing to the Lord,
> for he is highly exalted.
> The horse and its rider
> he has hurled into the sea." '
>
> *Exodus 15:19–21*

Moses and the people of Israel celebrated! The women sang, danced and played tambourines. Having seen the tremendous victories which God worked for them they instinctively erupted into rapturous praise. Those who have experienced much should praise much. Times of celebration and worship of God are integral to our walk with God. Our service of him should flow out of a life of worship. Praise, worship, celebration for the salvation he has brought us should be central to our life in God and not peripheral. They should always be part and parcel of our experience and not just an occasional happening.

The people of Israel celebrated God for who he is, as a person, not only for what he did for them. They gave God his 'worth' and took time off to appreciate and adore him. They found that words are inadequate to describe God's splendour, majesty and matchless beauty. They cried out, 'Who is like you – majestic in holiness, awesome in glory, working wonders?' (Exodus 15:11.) They stood together on the other side of the banks of the Red Sea absolutely overwhelmed by his greatness and excellence. They were 'lost in wonder, love and praise'. True worship springs from hearts that are truly captivated by a living revelation of the Lord, catching glimpses of him as he really is. Like John, if we really see him we too will fall down at his feet (Revelation 1:17). Sincere and true worship will be our spontaneous response.

True worship is not just a duty performed at appropriate times as part of a religious exercise, nor is it maintaining certain traditions and observing certain liturgy. It is not just a combination of mind and will-power which engage in cold, calculated and educated utterances. Neither is it mindless jabberings without any content. It is the whole person whose heart is melted in pure ecstasy and adoration, overcome by God's love and tender care, pouring itself out at his feet as though bathing them, as Mary did with her tears (John 12:1–8). We too must learn how to worship and celebrate truly, and so refresh and renew ourselves in order to be able to proceed on our journey with confidence.

The people also celebrated because of what God had done. They did not take the great deliverance, miracles and victories, triumph over their circumstances and their enemies for granted; they stopped to acknowledge that what they could not do in their own strength and power God did for them. What was utterly impossible God made possible. It was far more than they deserved. Unworthy and undeserving though we may be, that fact should not hinder us from appreciating what God has done for us. Our hearts burst forth with praise as a natural response when we see his mighty hand revealed in majestic power on our behalf.

Like the children of Israel we too must learn how to sing and dance and praise the Lord – our warrior, banner, healer and defender. He who watches over his own to protect them when the enemy pursues and when the floodwaters overflow, is there to give us his strength and to guide us to safety. 'The joy of the Lord is your strength' (Nehemiah 8:10). To him be all praise and honour and glory.

IN BITTER SITUATIONS

> 'Then Moses led Israel from the Red Sea and they went into the Desert of Shur. For three days they travelled in the desert without finding water. When they came to Marah, they could not drink its water because it was bitter. (That is why the place is called Marah.) So the people grumbled against Moses, saying, "What are we to drink?"
>
> Then Moses cried out to the Lord, and the Lord showed him a piece of wood. He threw it into the

> water, and the water became sweet.
>
> There the Lord made a decree and a law for them, and there he tested them. He said, "If you listen carefully to the voice of the Lord your God and do what is right in his eyes, if you pay attention to his commands and keep all his decrees, I will not bring on you any of the diseases I brought on the Egyptians, for I am the Lord who heals you." '
>
> *Exodus 15:22–26*

It seems odd that, after the exhilaration and high spirit of celebration at the Red Sea, Moses should lead Israel through the Wilderness of Shur to Marah. They went from the glorious atmosphere of celebration into the gruelling heat of the sun. Three days' hard journey. No water. Eventually they came to Marah and water, but alas their expectations were shattered. They found water but they could not drink it. It was bitter. Disappointment and hopelessness filled their hearts. Thirsty, dying for a drop of water to touch their parched lips and yet they could not because it was bitter. A pool of bitter water. The last thing they needed was more aggravation! How did they cope? God was there and he made all the difference.

Our pilgrimage will include coming across bitter waters. We encounter experiences which leave a bitter taste in our spirits, afflictions which leave us hurt and wounded. Unpleasant experiences with people often leave us feeling disillusioned, insulted and injured. It causes such pain that it rubs the smile off our faces, steals the joy of life. Such pain! Our bitter waters could be our impoverished resources when our own strength runs out and we are left dry, parched and barren, feeling utterly hopeless and unable to cope. It could be when we suffer want and need, longing that something will happen to alleviate the pressures and relieve our inward pain. It can be when we are misunderstood and our closest friends turn against us.

How do we cope in such bitter situations? What should we do? Well, we should definitely avoid the unhelpful example of the children of Israel! They were so undermined and disillusioned that they automatically murmured and complained. It seems that this reaction was a habit they couldn't break. They were professional complainers, always ready to believe the worst. They absorbed all that God gave but seemed to run out of faith when difficulty and adversity confronted them. They were cynical and sceptical, blaming everybody and anybody for their problems – except, of course, themselves. We may not be so different today; it is never our responsibility when things go wrong!

What a rotten and ugly attitude. Rather than fall into a deep pit of despair and faithlessness, allowing ourselves to be assailed with doubts and fears, we should turn to God in active faith, asking him to provide us with answers. Rather than allowing our faith to be undermined we should release our faith in God to work miracles. Faith in desperation always produces miracles. Doubt and despair mixed with murmurings and complainings is a sure recipe for disaster. Instead of allowing our anxieties to mount up and get the better of us, driving us to panic stations, we should release our energies God-ward and learn to rest in the loving care of our Father.

* * *

Rani was a lovely, vivacious teenager with a future full of promise. She came from a typical East Indian background and lived in a small village in South America. She accepted Christ and later answered the call of God to serve as a missionary. She met her tall, dark and handsome prince who was converted from Hinduism, also training to be a missionary. They fell deeply in love and resolved that they would serve the Lord together. Soon after their wedding they were sent out to their first mission field. The Lord blessed their ministry as they became involved in the pioneering of several churches. They had four lovely daughters. Their ministry assumed greater and greater proportions and he began to travel extensively to preach and conduct seminars for leaders. After many years of sacrificial labour they were beginning to set up a base for their work, which by this time extended into many countries, including Africa, India and the Caribbean.

Then the unexpected happened. They discovered cancer. He died two years later after intense suffering and pain leaving behind a young wife and four daughters who needed him more now than ever. Cut down in his prime. What do you say to a six-year-old girl when she asks with such earnest innocence, 'Why did Jesus take Daddy now?' Yet the five of them are a constant testimony and challenge to all who know them because they found strength in God, and continue to do so, as in all simplicity they reach out to the Lord to comfort them in their sorrow, to give them hope for the future and to provide for them financially.

* * *

Our metal will be tested in the fires of adversity. God

knew that at Marah the waters were bitter. It was no surprise to God, just as it was no surprise to God that Pharaoh and his armies pursued his people to destroy them. The arrival at Marah was no accident. The Lord instructed Moses to lead them there. It was all part of God's training and preparation for greater things. The experience was different from Pi Hahiroth but the purpose was the same. God always has an answer to our bitter situations. He does not want us to wallow in our misery. He told Moses to do a very simple, practical thing. To all appearances it was a rather insignificant gesture. 'The Lord showed him a piece of wood' which Moses then threw into the waters. Guess what!! The bitterness changed. The waters became sweet.

That tree which provided the wood must have lived long in their memory. To them it was an ordinary tree that God used to teach a very meaningful lesson and at the same time point them prophetically to an event of great significance. There is another tree to which the Lord directs our attention: the cross, the tree on which Jesus died and shed his precious blood. The cross marked a very bitter place for Jesus. It was the ultimate test of his loyalty to God and, as Jesus went through with it, God made his death the means of cleansing us from our guilt.

The Cross holds a strange mixture of suffering and grace. Jesus' suffering has brought God's grace to us. Our bitter experiences can be transformed by that grace. Our defeats can be turned into triumphs, our disillusionment into realisation of God's love and care, our grumbling and miserable moaning into thanksgiving and praise. The power that was at work in Jesus when God raised him from the dead, is there for us too. At times of testing we need to draw on that power to find grace to help us in our time of need (Hebrews 4:16). God's plan to redeem us fully and provide us with total salvation for the whole person was fulfilled when Jesus died and rose again.

Why testing?

It is very important that we do not lose sight of the whole purpose of the exercise; God never tests us for the pleasure of it or for the sake of it. He does not play games with us, there is always a good reason for what happens. Behind every test is an important lesson to be learnt. Each test contains a promise and a revelation of God's love and care for his people. See what the Israelites learnt from their test at Marah:

- That God will always remain faithful to his people even when things are parched, dry and impossible.
- That God is more than a match for our difficulties and problems; he can change our situation beyond all recognition, and beyond all our expectations.
- That complaining, murmuring, and blaming everybody else, does not pay. Being negative and pessimistic is not the way to bring lasting solutions. It is infantile behaviour.
- That God wanted to give them a prophetic vision of the Cross and show them a glimpse of things to come: that one day many will find an answer for the bitterness which sin and Satan have inflicted on humanity; that all thirsty souls will find satisfaction if they come and drink from the sweet waters that flow from the wells of salvation (see Isaiah 12:1–3).

What, then, was the promise? That none of the judgements that fell on the unrepentant Egyptians would fall on them and that, on the contrary, the Lord would continue to heal them and make them whole. But the promise was conditional in that God required commitment on their part. They were to 'listen carefully to the voice of the Lord . . . do what is right in his eyes . . . pay attention to his commands and keep all his decrees' (Exodus 15:26).

We cannot expect God to keep his promise to us if we continually rebel, disobey and do things our own way without any regard to his will and pleasure. We are saved by faith, but to live under the blessings of God, obedience is a must. As Peter put it: 'We have been chosen . . . for obedience to Jesus Christ' (1 Peter 1:2).

What then was the revelation? Every time God meets and deals with his people he leaves them with a fresh revelation of himself. He is always looking for an opportunity to communicate himself to us, to show us something more about himself and his relationship to us. The revelation God gave the Israelites here was of a God who cares and a God who can. 'I am the Lord who heals you.' God cares. He thinks about our welfare and is deeply concerned that we should not live with our bitterness. Rather he desires to reverse our situation and to turn every bitter pool in our lives into the sweetness of his grace. He is interested and wants to work for our healing and victory. And he wants to do so in order to attract other people to him. Paul writes: 'Thanks be to God, who always leads us in triumphant procession in Christ and through us spreads everywhere the fragrance of the knowledge of him' (2

Corinthians 2:14).

God always has our welfare and best interest at heart. We are the object of his love, the apple of his eye, the centre of his care, the darling of his heart. And, surprisingly, this is so even when we act stupidly and respond all wrongly. His love for us is not dependent on our performance. He loves us for his own sake.

ENJOYING GOD'S ABUNDANCE

> 'Then they came to Elim, where there were twelve springs and seventy palm trees, and they camped there near the water.' Exodus 15:27

From Marah to Elim, from the scorching desert sun to an oasis in the desert, from tired wearisome journeying to a place of shade and quiet rest. God moved them on from one thing to another. There was time for relaxation and rest, for refreshing and recreation but no room for getting stuck in the mud or becoming stagnant. With each new experience comes a new lesson of faith. With every mile covered they were drawn nearer to God and closer to their final destination. They came from Marah – Bitter Waters – to Elim, a place of rest, shade and plenty. Written into God's design for his people are regular interludes of retreat, to withdraw from the heat of battle in order to give time for renewal and revival.

Marah is never the place to set up camp. It was meant to be a transitory encounter – an interval, not a place for any permanent dwelling. God never intends the bitter experiences in our lives to have any kind of permanence.

And so God led them to Elim, a very different scenario altogether. The pilgrim is ever pressing forward not willing to settle but always reaching for more. Contrary to the opinion of some, God's chosen path for us is also filled with happy, joyful, hilarious occasions. Positive happenings. It is not one long series of testings and trials. Praise God! What a lovely place Elim must have been. No one murmured here, no one expressed anything negative, no one seemed to miss the smoke of the brick kilns of Egypt.

Elim was a beautiful, large oasis in the middle of the desert sand. A clear blue sky by day and a million twinkling stars by night to provide a canopy for bubbling springs and picturesque palm trees. An ideal place to settle in the midst of surrounding hot, brown sand. What a welcome sight it must have been after the fatigue and weariness of trekking for days through the wilderness. Twelve springs of fresh, drinkable water! Enough so that each tribe could have a well all to themselves! No need for quarrelling. No cause for competition. Seventy date palms which provided enough food and shade: an idyllic setting suitable for weary travellers to enjoy.

Like the children of Israel we also need to come away from the difficult testing times to renew our strength in quiet aloneness with God. For we too become weary and tired. Our drooping spirits need to be revived. We need to enjoy the waters of the wells of salvation, to have times of retreat. Away from the pressures of life and the heat of testings we can experience the springing up, the inner flow, of our new life in Christ. Jesus said to the woman of Samaria, who was desperate, lonely and in need: 'the water I give him will become in him a spring of water, welling up to eternal life' (John 4:14).

How we need to spend time waiting on the Lord, lingering in his presence! We need to take time to drink our fill, until our thirsty souls are soaked and immersed in the Holy Spirit. ' "If a man is thirsty," Jesus said, "let him come to me and drink. Whoever believes in me, as the Scripture has said, streams of living water will flow from within him." By this he meant the Spirit' (John 7:37–39). What a thrill that out of our innermost being *streams*, not just *a* stream, but streams of living waters can flow! Fortified in our inner self by the great power of the Holy Spirit working deep in our own hearts, we can resume our journey with new courage and confidence. God has provided rich blessings for us in such abundance! Let us enjoy them by faith and no longer hold back. God is a good God and he does not skimp on our salvation (see Ephesians 1:3). Yet some Christians endure their walk with God instead of enjoying it.

Let us come and pitch our tent beside the waters as they did. Find your personal Elim, a place where God can meet with you at regular intervals; a time and place when you can enjoy his love and grace. It is worth enduring the testing times because we know that it is only for a season. The time soon comes when the Lord meets with us to heal our wounds, refresh our souls and renew our strength so that we can go on further in our pilgrimage. We may well survive without these times of refreshing, but it will be a dull and dreary struggle and the chances are we will become stagnated and stultified. We may even perish on the way.

* * *

Oba sat in the class with his colleagues, staring blankly with a distant look in his eyes, the kind which tells you a whole lot more than words can express. It was the sort of look which says, 'I'm trying, but I find it difficult to cope. I can't make it.' He was a rough teenager in a gang from one of the worst parts of the city. Two years earlier the Lord had met with him wonderfully, and delivered him. He experienced such a complete change of heart that he became the talk of the community. After his conversion, Oba felt the Lord's call on his life to be a missionary, and he responded readily and positively with no hesitation. Unfortunately, it was not long before he began to have one trial after another, one test followed hard on the heels of the last one. He was left perplexed, weak and tired and now, here he sat in the midst of his colleagues thinking, 'I can't go on, it's too much.'

We discerned what was happening and offered to pray with him. After some time in prayer and worship we felt that we should lay hands on our brother and ask the Lord to remove the tiredness from his spirit and release him from the weariness of soul. There was such a cloud of heaviness on Oba and we prayed earnestly until we sensed the Holy Spirit lifting the heaviness and flooding him with peace and joy. He began to praise the Lord softly at first but, as he experienced wave after wave of God's river of love washing over him, he became free and more fluent in his praises. It was obvious the Holy Spirit was working deep within to renew his confidence, which was badly bruised, and to restore his joy.

He arose from that moment refreshed, the gloom and weight of the many months suddenly lifted. He was a different person. In the ensuing weeks he spent time in prayer and fasting which brought him into closer fellowship and intimacy with the Lord, sealing his victory. He subsequently finished his training. Now, happily married, he is serving the Lord as a pioneer missionary in a small nation in Central America.

* * *

If you are feeling weary, tired, worn and bruised there is a place where you too can meet with the Lord and be refreshed. Stop where you are and allow the Holy Spirit to minister to you. Rivers of living water will flow again. Maybe your faith has been undermined, assailed with doubts and fears, your confidence dented. Do not put on a brave face and pretend that all is well. Find your Elim. God is waiting there, the Holy Spirit stands ready to touch you at the point of your need and fill you with his peace, reassurance and joy again. Again and again we need such times of meeting with God to receive his ministry and help in our pilgrim journey. Elim – what a blessed place to be at!

6

WHEN THE GOING GETS TOUGH

I am sure the people of Israel were feeling quite relaxed at Elim and even entertained thoughts of settling down there. After all, they were far away from Egypt now. No need to fear. They had liberty and it was lovely there. They had all they needed. There was even scope for development. But the time had come again for them to move on. When the order came from Moses to pull up stakes and set out, I imagine they were not very pleased. I can almost hear them muttering under their breath, 'Not again!'

> 'The whole Israelite community set out from Elim and came to the Desert of Sin, which is between Elim and Sinai, on the fifteenth day of the second month after they had come out of Egypt. In the desert the whole community grumbled against Moses and Aaron. The Israelites said to them, "If only we had died by the Lord's hand in Egypt! There we sat

> round pots of meat and ate all the food we wanted, but you have brought us out into this desert to starve this entire assembly to death." ' *Exodus 16:1–3*

You can almost hear their reasoning, can't you? It is not a natural human response to want to take unnecessary risks and step out into uncharted territory. Not if you can help it. Just as they cried out earlier when they faced destruction by Pharaoh, I guess they were saying at Elim, 'Leave us alone here to settle.'

Peter, James and John felt exactly the same when they were on the mountain top away from the problems and difficulties in the valley. There they saw Jesus, revealed before their very eyes in all his brilliance and glory (Matthew 17:1–13). The atmosphere was charged with divine presence and energy. They felt good and thoroughly blessed. They had a little foretaste of the glory that awaits us all who truly love and believe in Jesus. So in their naïvete they made a sincere and impassioned plea, 'Lord, let us build tents here.' I can imagine a paraphrased reply from the Lord. 'How can you ask such a thing of me? Don't you understand anything? My mission is not yet fulfilled, my own pilgrimage has a way yet to go, and so has yours for that matter. Come on, let's go down. There is an epileptic boy at the foot of the mountain waiting for us. There are some more demons to be cast out, some more accusations to face, a cross to bear, a resurrection yet to come. Now is not the time to settle in this charismatic atmosphere.' So it is that just when we feel good and comfortable, we are called upon to move on deeper and further into the purpose of God.

The next stop for the children of Israel was Sinai

where God was waiting to do greater things, to give them commandments and instructions that would eventually help them to be organised into a nation. What a great day awaited them!

En route to Sinai they had to pass through another wilderness. From the shady oasis of Elim through the wilderness of Sin. And wouldn't you know it? This time they ran out of food. Try as they must have done, they could not see how it was humanly possible to meet this need. How could they get food in this desert? They got to the point where they didn't know where their next meal would come from. Imagine the scene. Children, men and women stranded in the vast wilderness, hungry and starving. Nothing demoralises a person more than to stand by helplessly and see his children go hungry. They must have thought that Moses did not know what he was doing. 'Why didn't we stay at Elim?' The thought must often have crossed their minds.

Another test, another opportunity to prove God. What did they do? They panicked again. You would have thought they might have learnt something from their past experiences, but it seems as though history taught them nothing. Surely they must know by now that God will not let them down? They saw God work tremendous miracles in Egypt. They witnessed how the Lord stood up for them, defending them against the Egyptians. They could not have forgotten how he delivered them from bondage, how he caused them to triumph and destroy all Pharaoh's armies. Yet, what did they do? Did they call on the Lord? Did they sing praises? No. You guessed right. Instead, they grumbled, complained, fretted and carried on as people who had never seen God work, as those that do not know him.

We know God can do great things. He has even helped *us* in the past. He has proved his love and faithfulness again and again – yet, when faced with difficulties and problems, we tend to forget that. We revert to type . . . grumble, grumble, grumble. We can be so faithless, and sometimes very ungrateful people. Problems. We have them as well, don't we? Sometimes quite impossible situations. We don't know how we will manage to pay our bills, cope with our marriage, control the children. We face moral problems, relationship problems, career problems; problems of scarcity, bankruptcy, mortgage, unemployment – even church problems. We get locked into difficult corners or fall on hard times.

How should we react under adverse conditions? Let us not repeat the mistakes of the Israelites. Getting anxious, worrying and fretting solves nothing – it only increases our blood pressure. We know the Lord will not let us down if we put our trust in him. Take courage my friend! It is written, 'The one who trusts in him will never be put to shame' (Romans 9:33).

In spite of their pessimism and unbelief the Lord provided manna for the children of Israel. Right there in an empty barren wasteland where nothing grows he did the impossible. He gave them food. He will provide for us also. His name is *El-Shaddai*, our all sufficiency. The God of miracles lives!

> 'Then the Lord said to Moses, "I will rain down bread from heaven for you. The people are to go out each day and gather enough for that day. In this way I will test them and see whether they will follow my instructions. On the sixth day they are to prepare

> what they bring in, and that is to be twice as much as they gather on the other days."
>
> . . . The Israelites did as they were told; some gathered much, some little. And when they measured it by the omer, he who gathered much did not have too much, and he who gathered little did not have too little.
>
> . . . The Israelites ate manna for forty years, until they came to a land that was settled; they ate manna until they reached the border of Canaan.'
>
> *Exodus 16:4–5, 17–18, 35*

To provide manna was God's responsibility, to collect it was the direct responsibility of the people. To benefit from God's provision requires diligent, positive action. Like them we too must reach out in faith and make the effort to gather into our store his rich supply. Sometimes we are too lazy. We lack discipline or initiative. All too often we do not even try to find the things so crucial for our spiritual health and growth. Instead, we get involved with things that do not contribute to our growth in God. 'Go out and gather your daily manna so that you will have enough,' was the instruction. 'Gather it morning by morning, every person as much as he can eat, for when the sun grows hot it will be gone.' Don't sit and wait. It will not drop into your lap! It's not automatic.

It takes effort on our part to discipline ourselves to seek God and learn for ourselves how to feed on the living bread, Christ. We cannot afford to lean on other people. We cannot stumble through life leaning on crutches. Peter said, 'Long for pure milk of the Lord for by it you may grow in respect to your salvation.' (1 Peter

2:2, NASB; see also Psalm 1:2–3; Ephesians 5:26; John 17:17.) To feed daily on the word of God is as essential to our development in God as regular prayer. Read it, read it again, write it down, pray it in, do it and pass it on. These are the simple golden rules which, if practised regularly, will establish, strengthen and equip you to stand firm, especially in times of severe testing.

A JOURNEY IN STAGES

> 'The whole Israelite community set out from the Desert of Sin, travelling from place to place as the Lord commanded.' *Exodus 17:1*

God does not expect us to reach our destination in one gigantic leap. The Lord understands us better than we know ourselves. He knows how much our feeble frame can bear. He understands that we have limited capacity and are only able to absorb so much at any given time. The Lord will not push us beyond the limit of our endurance (see 1 Corinthians 10:13). We sometimes overestimate that limit and may push ourselves too far, much to our hurt. Knowing us as he does he leads us one step at a time into his purpose for our lives. We cannot do better for ourselves than to keep in the perfect will of God. To walk in step with God as he commands is the only guarantee that we will reach the destination which he has in his wisdom preordained for us: 'The Lord delights in the way of the man whose steps he has made firm; though he stumble, he will not fall, for the Lord upholds him with his hand' (Psalm 37:23–24).

Not only do we need to discover God's chosen path

for us, but it is also vital to discover the pace at which we should pursue his will. It is reasonable to suppose that many of the Israelites would have liked to move in one swift movement from Egypt directly into the land of Caanan without any of the hassles, difficulties or problems of the round-about route. We too, like them, must learn that real life is never like that. It is a discipline, building brick by brick, one upon another, taking one step at a time. Some of our steps may be faltering. Sometimes in our impetuosity and impatience we run ahead of God. If you are anything like me you even wish that everything was done yesterday. When we try to get ahead like this we only run into a brick wall.

There are also those who lag behind. They are equally in danger of missing God. They live in the past, they get buried in their traditions and are too lazy to stir themselves. They do not care enough to find out if God is saying or doing anything new or different. They live in a past that bears no relevance to the present. The Holy Spirit can be doing things right in front of them and they would not even notice.

We may never know all that is in store for us but at least we should do our best to make sure that what we are doing in the present is in the centre of God's will. To drift aimlessly along, hoping for the best, is irresponsible to say the least. There are times when everything appears to come to a dead end. But it has been proved by many through the years that our obedience is often the key that opens the door into the next phase.

WHEN DISASTER STRIKES

> 'They camped at Rephidim, but there was no water for the people to drink. So they quarrelled with Moses and said, 'Give us water to drink.'
>
> Moses replied, "Why do you quarrel with me? Why do you put the Lord to the test?"
>
> But the people were thirsty for water there, and they grumbled against Moses. They said, "Why did you bring us up out of Egypt to make us and our children and livestock die of thirst?"
>
> . . . The Israelites quarrelled and . . . tested the Lord saying, "Is the Lord among us or not?" '
>
> *Exodus 17:1–3, 7*

Again, Israel was faced with a problem. They arrived at Rephidim and found there was no water for the people to drink. No question about it: it was no easy situation. Water is essential. Without it men, women, children and cattle will die. Serious; very serious. How did they react? Once again, instead of looking to the Lord who sustained them and intervened so many times, and who had miraculously provided all they needed so far, they reacted wrongly and behaved miserably. Obviously, they did not learn the lessons that God was trying to teach them at the Red Sea, Marah, Elim and in the wilderness of Sin. He had so graciously and abundantly provided for them that, just for once, they could have showed some confidence in him, given God some credit for being God.

Instead the people quarrelled and grumbled as they had umpteen times before. Nothing had really changed in their basic attitude despite all they had seen of God's grace and goodness. Their motto was, 'Nothing changes here!' They still did not know how to cope in times of crisis and difficulty. 'Give us water,' they demanded. No sense of gratitude.

Their thirst for water was legitimate, and they really were in a desperate situation. But there is no excuse for a people who have received so much to call into question God's good intention and loving care for them. Yet their discontent and distrust grew so deep and intense that they could bottle it up no longer. Their impatience got the better of them and eventually erupted in a passionate and violent reaction against God and Moses. They had allowed circumstances to undermine their confidence in God to such a degree that they questioned whether all that had happened to them in the past had anything at all to do with God. In effect, they were challenging God to show himself; to prove, by working a miracle, that he really was with them still. What a state of affairs. *They* dared to test Almighty *God*. Wow! They concluded that the long series of signs and wonders and endless miracles, which had served them so well and led to their deliverance, were probably a big hoax.

They had got to the point of being willing to throw away all they possessed in God and in so doing put their entire future at risk. They were ready to jeopardise their covenant partnership with God which he had planned to lead to the redemption of the whole human race.

People have not changed much. There are many parallels in our time. We too have struggles and problems when faced with hard questions and difficulties, questions to which we cannot easily find answers. When the pressure gets too much and there seems no way out, we usually behave just as miserably, negatively and carnally as they did. Sometimes, the more we pray the harder it gets. We stumble, feel hurt, and wonder why our prayers are not answered.

This question of pain and disappointment remains a mystery. Why should the righteous suffer when the wicked prosper? Why should young children be left without parents, young men and women cut down in the prime of their youth by some accident or illness? Why should a mother and children be left without a father who loved and cared for them? Questions like these bombard our minds almost daily and, if we let them, they can undermine our confidence in God and throw us off balance. Why do some people stay sick when they believed God was going to heal them? These are hard questions.

There are no easy answers. We need to admit that we do not know everything, that we sometimes have no answer. People can often accept and understand this more easily than our pretending that we do know. It does not help to give casual, simplistic answers. Besides being insensitive to the feelings and emotions of those suffering, and insulting their intelligence, they do God very little credit. If we are honest, we realise with Paul that we only 'know in part' and we can only prophesy and counsel in part (1 Corinthians 13:9). We cannot know for sure exactly what God is doing in our lives or in anyone else's. 'Who has known the mind of the Lord? Or who has been his counsellor?' asks Paul. He speaks of 'the depth of the riches of the wisdom and knowledge of God . . . How undescribable his judgements, and his paths beyond tracing out' (Romans 11:33–34).

So, whatever our circumstances – and even despite them – the best thing to do is to summon up the last ounce of our faith and rise above the doubts and fears that press upon us. Trust God in spite of everything. Trust him to grant you the strength and grace to deliver and sustain you. As one great saint of God said, 'God grant me the serenity to accept the things I cannot change, courage to change the things I can, and wisdom to know the difference.'

Should we not ask questions, then, when we are perplexed? Of course we should. God is not austere and unreasonable. It is healthy to ask why something is happening; God did not create us to be mindless and unthinking. He has respect for an enquiring mind and will give regard to those who seek a reason for their problems.

But is it fair to *blame* all our misfortunes on God? Is it right to lay the fault on God's doorstep? The people of Israel did not only question God, they blamed him. Their real grouse was not really with Moses but God. We sometimes tend to forget the real cause of our problems; we do not like to accept that the real root of all that threatens to overwhelm and destroy us is sin. Sin both separates us from God and leaves us very vulnerable to the attacks of Satan. This is not a very popular way to think in our modern society but, with all the sophistication, advanced knowledge and psychology of our time, we have not produced any better answers. We blame society, our environment, our past, everybody and anybody apart from ourselves. We need to face up to a question ourselves: what responsibility do *I* bear for bringing about this situation?

In some cases of suffering and confusion about the

way ahead there is a real element of mystery which we cannot deny. The cause cannot be immediately traced. Explanations only help to complicate matters. We don't know all the factors involved. But there are three things which we can know and of which we can be assured:

- We know that not every disaster that befalls us is directly attributable to some personal individual sin. The fact is that we live in a sinful world. Sinfulness and evil permeate society. This world is greatly influenced by the devil – 'the ruler of the kingdom of the air . . . who is now at work in those who are disobedient' (Ephesians 2:2).
- We know that God does not abandon or forsake us. He really does care and is concerned for us even in the very minute details of our lives. What happens to us is his heart concern. We sometimes have to accept that our suffering cannot be avoided but that the Lord has made provision for us in it. 'My grace is sufficient for you,' the Lord said to Paul, 'for my power is made perfect in weakness' (2 Corinthians 12:9). And in Proverbs we read: 'Trust in the Lord with all your heart and lean not on your own understanding; in all your ways acknowledge him, and he will make your paths straight. Do not be wise in your own eyes; fear the Lord and shun evil. This will bring health to your body and nourishment to your bones' (Proverbs 3:5–8).
- We know that the Lord has promised that a great day is coming when everything will be straightened out and put right. Those who have done wrong will be judged, those who have done right will be rewarded, and those who have suffered unjustly will be healed. Every cloudy situation will be made clear and everyone

will receive their just dessert.

It is sometimes hard to believe that a man like David had similar doubts and questions. He devoted a whole Psalm to wrestling with them and came up with some answers which we would do well to consider (see Psalm 37). When the children of Israel were faced with that apparent dead-end at Rephidim, they, too, would have done well to sit down and contemplate their God as David did. If you feel that disaster has struck, that there is no way forward and no way back, I urge you to read that Psalm and allow the Lord to bring you assurance, comfort and counsel.

WATER FROM THE ROCK

> Then Moses cried out to the Lord, 'What am I to do with these people? They are almost ready to stone me.'
>
> The Lord answered Moses, 'Walk on ahead of the people. Take with you some of the elders of Israel and take in your hand the staff with which you struck the Nile, and go. I will stand there before you by the rock at Horeb. Strike the rock, and water will come out of it for the people to drink.' So Moses did this in the sight of the elders of Israel. And he called the place Massah and Meribah because the Israelites quarrelled and because they tested the Lord saying, 'Is the Lord among us or not?'
>
> *Exodus 17:4–7*

The patience and love of God towards us is truly amazing. Even though the children of Israel had behaved so disagreeably God still heard their grumbles, listened to the cry of their hearts and saw their need. God knew that the rock was there and he knew what he wanted to do. He wanted not only to give them water but to show them something that would have significance for all peoples far beyond their own time and generation. They completely missed it, the highlight of the whole event. Water is used in the scriptures to symbolise the word of God, life of God and the Spirit of God. The water which flowed in a river from that rock was not just to satisfy their immediate thirst, but to symbolise the refreshing, life-giving presence of God among them. Their question, 'Is the Lord among us or not?' was answered.

God intended them to be a living witness to nations around that life and blessing were to be found only in him, but because they lacked spiritual perception they failed in their calling to be that witness.

This incident was also full of prophetic symbolism. When Paul referred to it he drew out its wider significance and also included a warning to those of us who now follow Christ:

> 'For I do not want you to be ignorant of the fact, brothers, that our forefathers were all under the cloud and that they all passed through the sea. They were all baptised into Moses in the cloud and in the sea. They all ate the same spiritual food and drank the same spiritual drink; for they drank from the spiritual rock that accompanied them, and that rock was Christ. Nevertheless, God was not pleased with most of them; their bodies were scattered over the desert.

> Now these things occurred as examples, to keep us from setting our hearts on evil things as they did . . . We should not test the Lord as some of them did – and were killed by snakes. And do not grumble, as some of them did – and were killed by the destroying angel.
>
> These things happened to them as examples and were written down as warnings for us on whom the fulfilment of the ages has come. So, if you think you are standing firm, be careful that you don't fall! No temptation has seized you except what is common to man. And God is faithful; he will not let you be tempted beyond what you can bear. But when you are tempted, he will also provide a way out so that you can stand up under it.'
>
> *1 Corinthians 10:1–6, 9–13*

God wanted the people of Israel to catch a glimpse of the future and to symbolise the situation of all who will believe and come to Christ. The rock symbolises Christ, out of whom living water flows for all humanity for all time. Jesus said, ' "If a man is thirsty, let him come to me and drink. Whoever believes in me, as the Scripture has said, streams of living water will flow from within him." By this he meant that Spirit, whom those who believed in him were later to receive' (John 7:37–39).

We do well to listen to the words of the great apostle Paul and to learn our lesson if we want to progress in God's purpose for us. Our rock, Jesus Christ, was struck by the rod of God when he hung on the cross, so opening up a fountain of spiritually pure, refreshing water. That rock is still flowing with living water. Let us come and drink with hearts full of gratitude and thanksgiving.

It is not enough to have a drink at Marah or Elim, the occasional once in a few days; we need to drink of the Spirit daily. God didn't just give them a cupful of water each; he gave them a whole river which flowed on and on! They need not be thirsty *any more!* We have the unlimited resources of God available to us, so let us drink and be full of his Spirit. In spite of all that happens in our lives, and all the mistakes that we make, God doesn't take away from us the availability of his Spirit. It is our source of life, joy and power. So often we feel spiritually dry – often when we're feeling low anyway – cut off from God, thinking we might have sinned against him. If we only have the good sense to return to the source and clear up the rubbish blocking its flow, we will find that the supply of living waters is still there.

SPIRITUAL WARFARE

> 'The Amalekites came and attacked the Israelites at Rephidim. Moses said to Joshua, "Choose some of our men and go out to fight the Amalekites. Tomorrow I will stand on top of the hill with the staff of God in my hands."
>
> So Joshua fought the Amalekites as Moses had ordered, and Moses, Aaron and Hur went to the top of the hill. As long as Moses held up his hands, the Israelites were winning, but whenever he lowered his hands, the Amalekites were winning. When Moses' hands grew tired, they took a stone and put it under him and he sat on it. Aaron and Hur held his hands up – one on one side, one on

> the other – so that his hands remained steady till sunset. So Joshua overcame the Amalekite army with the sword.
>
> Then the Lord said to Moses, "Write this on a scroll as something to be remembered and make sure that Joshua hears it, because I will completely erase the memory of the Amalekites from under heaven."
>
> Moses built an altar and called it, The Lord is my Banner. He said, "For hands were lifted up to the throne of the Lord. The Lord will be at war against the Amalekites from generation to generation." '
>
> *Exodus 17:8–16*

'The Amalekites came and attacked the Israelites at Rephidim.' Sounds familiar? The enemy does not give up without a fight! Defeated in Egypt he pursued them to the Red Sea and here once again at Rephidim he launched another attack on Israel. A different place, a different king and a different army. Israel probably thought that having overcome Pharaoh and his armies they could now sail through without any further battles. Sorry, disappointment!

Running right through the story of Israel is one attack after the other, each one designed to frustrate and defeat them. They occurred with frightening regularity, hardly giving them the chance to get their breath back.

Besides that of the persistence of the enemy, there is another important lesson to be learnt from this story: war was waged on two fronts. Joshua was fighting with the soldiers at ground level while Moses, Aaron and Hur were waging warfare at another level. Israel only prevailed because warfare was done in the heavenly realms and when they prevailed in the heavenly realms so Joshua also prevailed on the ground. Paul wrote, 'Our struggle is not against flesh and blood, but against the rulers, against the authorities, against the powers of this dark world and against the spiritual forces of evil in the heavenly realms' (Ephesians 6:10). And Peter warned that, 'Your enemy the devil prowls around like a roaring lion looking for someone to devour. Resist him, standing firm in the faith' (1 Peter 5:8–9).

The very first promise of salvation that God gave, foretold this struggle. In the Garden of Eden, the Lord said that there would be enmity between the serpent who deceived Eve, and the offspring of Eve – Christ. And our salvation would come through Christ's defeat of the serpent. When we accepted Christ and decided to follow him we therefore declared war against the enemy and he has declared war against us. To prevail in the battles that result, we need to learn the art of spiritual warfare in heavenly places. If we are to fulfil our mission as the people of God – to bring others into his kingdom too – then we must attack and invade the strongholds of Satan here on earth. Intercession on one hand, evangelism on the other. 'Though we live in the world we do not wage war as the world does. The weapons we fight with are not the weapons of the world. On the contrary, they have divine power to demolish strongholds. We demolish arguments and every pretension that sets itself up against the knowledge of God' (2 Corinthians 10:3–5). We need to get down to serious business, to pray earnestly, and with fasting, against all the Amalekites of this world, that God will intervene and set people free from the power of the enemy. Being a pilgrim is knowing how to fight on our knees as well as on our feet.

God does not leave us to fend for ourselves against the attacks of the enemy. There are particular ways in which he prepares us for it and works with us in it:

- He pinpoints those wrong attitudes and weaknesses that are buried deep in our hearts.
- He then guides us into situations where those previously hidden things that hinder our spiritual growth and development, are exposed.
- He then proceeds to deal with them, helping us to work through any unresolved issues that hinder our progress.
- He leads us to confession and repentance of any sin, that we may be cleansed.
- He inspires and energises our prayers and intercession, by the Holy Spirit.

We know that the God who intervened on behalf of the Israelites at Rephidim is the same God who is on our side. As we fight, he fights. Let us not therefore lose heart when we are tried. Let us not throw away our confidence in God or lose our eternal perspective for, as Paul says, 'our light and momentary troubles are achieving for us an eternal glory that far outweighs them all. So we fix our eyes not on what is seen, but on what is unseen. For what is seen is temporary, but what is unseen is eternal' (2 Cor 4:17–18). 'In times of great distress when the pressures of life would seem to squeeze us out of measure let us look unto Jesus who is the author and finisher of our faith' (Hebrews 12:1–2, NASB).

7

STAGNATION

At last came the time all the people had been waiting for; their journeys had brought them to the borders of the Promised Land, Canaan:

> 'The Lord said to Moses, "Send some men to explore the land of Canaan, which I am giving to the Israelites. From each ancestral tribe send one of its leaders."
>
> So at the Lord's command Moses sent them out from the Desert of Paran . . .
>
> They came back to Moses and Aaron and the whole Israelite community at Kadesh in the Desert of Paran. There they reported to them and to the whole assembly and showed them the fruit of the land. They gave Moses this account: "We went into the land to which you sent us, and it does flow with milk and honey! Here is its fruit. But the people who live there are powerful, and the cities are fortified and very large . . ."

> And they spread among the Israelites a bad report about the land they had explored. They said, "The land we explored devours those living in it. All the people we saw there are of great size."
>
> That night all the people of the community raised their voices and wept aloud. All the Israelites grumbled against Moses and Aaron, and the whole assembly said to them, "If only we had died in Egypt! Or in this desert! Why is the Lord bringing us to this land only to let us fall by the sword? Our wives and children will be taken as plunder. Wouldn't it be better for us to go back to Egypt?" And they said to each other, "We should choose a leader and go back to Egypt." '
>
> *Numbers 13: 1–3, 26–28, 32; 14: 1–5*

There was something very tragic about the people of Israel. They rejoiced, celebrated, were very excited to leave Egypt, crossed the Red Sea, experienced deliverance, witnessed spectacular miracles, saw the hand of God demonstrated in mighty power against all their enemies, and received and lived in the good of all God's best gifts. Yet when God brought them to their destination, the reason for all he had done and all they had gone through, they flatly refused to go in.

It is amazing that people who had seen and experienced so much were unwilling to yield fully to God. It didn't even seem to cross their minds that they might be able to trust him again. And because of their lack of submission they forfeited his plan for them. Who would have thought that a people who came out with such triumph would have ended up free from Pharaoh but lost in the wilderness and to the purposes of God? Because they were unwilling to press ahead into the

Promised Land, they carried on wandering for forty whole years:

> 'The Lord said to Moses and Aaron, "How long will this wicked community grumble against me? I have heard the complaints of these grumbling Israelites. So tell them, 'As surely as I live, declares the Lord, I will do to you the very things I heard you say: In this desert your bodies will fall – every one of you twenty years old or more . . . Not one of you will enter the land I swore with uplifted hand to make your home, except Caleb son of Jephunneh and Joshua son of Nun. As for your children that you said would be taken as plunder, I will bring them in to enjoy the land you have rejected. But you – your bodies will fall in this desert. Your children will be shepherds here for forty years . . . one year for each of the forty days you explored the land.' " '
>
> *Numbers 14: 26–34*

How sad that they spent forty long years wandering in the wilderness – a desert place, dry, barren, difficult – going round and round in circles. Their progress halted, they became stagnant. Stuck. How sad that the very people who embraced and enjoyed the blessings of deliverance could not embrace and accept the discipline necessary for them to succeed in the purposes of God. Tragic indeed. Surely God did not bring them out of Pharoah's Egypt to leave them to wander around in a desert wilderness? A journey of forty days took forty *years*. Why? God's desire was for them to pass through the wilderness, not for their bones to be buried there. His call was to come into the Promised Land. Someone has said, 'it was a lot easier for God to bring them out of Egypt than to take Egypt out of them.' They missed God because they did not submit to God or his servant Moses. They were stubborn and hard-hearted, inflexible, unteachable and disobedient. They wanted their own way.

There are many Christians in a similar situation in our time. They are willing to go so far but no further. They do not go far enough with God. They restrict God by the limitations they put upon themselves, by their own unwillingness to embrace the dealings of God in their lives.

* * *

Santano was muscular, strong, full of daring and courage. Whenever he was with me I felt we could tackle anything, tame the jungle, build a building, pioneer a church, whether in the worst part of the city or primitive jungle village! I confess he gave me courage and lent me his strength. He feared nothing and had enough faith for both of us. He commanded the respect of his peers whether in matters spiritual or practical. He was a born leader.

But he had a problem. He could lead a team but could not work with a team; he had to do it his way. He preached with power, cast out demons without any fear, healed the sick. Through his preaching and counselling we saw many youths who had been hooked on drugs changed and rehabilitated. He would get into an area where everyone else had failed, and he would succeed. He had difficulty with leadership. He was kind yet obstinate, gentle but cruel, friendly yet frightening. And there was another problem. He could not accept criticism. All my love and prayerful counsel would be accepted if I did not correct him. A strong unyielding will! Try as I may I could not get him to see his faults. He would go so far, but when it came to the crucial point of surrendering his will to the Lord, he would go no further.

Many tried to help, and he too would try, but I could see that he was not really willing to make the necessary change, to sacrifice and surrender his will. Eventually his character got the better of him and his decline was so rapid it became a matter of great sadness and loss to all, not least to me. I still weep. He had so much promise.

* * *

The circumstances and the geography may be different for us today, but there are still many who show such promise when they accept Christ but, after a time, get stuck. They level off. They find it difficult to leave the elementary, baby-stage of faith and press on to maturity (see Hebrews 6: 1). They can only feed on milk. These people have been wonderfully delivered from sin and Satan. They have received many answers to prayer, even seen miracles, yet they cannot go beyond a certain point. They reach ceiling far too soon. Their prayer life dries up. Some settle down, become indifferent, even give up trying. Like the children of Israel, they enjoy the blessings but refuse the disciplines necessary for growth and maturity. We are willing to receive but not willing to learn.

The first lesson for any disciple of Jesus is the willingness to learn of him. 'Come to me, all you who are weary and burdened, and I will give you rest. Take my yoke upon you and learn from me, for I am gentle and humble in heart, and you will find rest for your souls. For my yoke is easy and my burden is light' (Matthew 11: 28–30). Here we have in Jesus' own words two golden rules, twin secrets if you like, so essential if we are to come into God's fulness. They are: Come and Receive, and Submit and Learn. To receive involves the exercise of faith. To learn involves the practice of obedience. Receiving by faith is done in only a moment but learning by obedience takes time, a whole lifetime.

'We must not lay again the first foundations but we must go on to perfection' (Hebrews 6: 1, NASB). 'Perfection' here means to complete according to plan, to finish the process. In other words, leave the infancy stages; grow up. Allow God to finish the good work which he started in you. Go on to maturity, completeness, wholeness.

This is the real challenge. To permit God to bring us out of our past, but also bring us into our future. To bring us out of our hurts but also bring us into healing. To bring us out of our bondages but also bring us into freedom. To bring us out of our brokenness into his wholeness. This is our inheritance. That is why Jesus died. So let us leave the elementary class and press on to maturity.

It is time for us to lift up our heads and set our sights on higher things, better things. Things more glorious, more exciting, more challenging, more demanding. Let us not stop short, satisfied to stay on the beaches with our toes in the water. Let us rather venture into the deep with God, cut our shore lines and abandon ourselves to follow wherever the Lord leads.

MISSING OUT ON GOD

Why did the children of Israel miss out on God? Here are some points to consider. They will encourage us, as well as challenge us to come out of our apathy and indifference. Let us determine in our hearts not to become casualties and liabilities of the kingdom, never to be a people on whom the grace of God is wasted, whose bones will lie buried in the sands of time. Instead, let us resolve to stand up and be counted. In spite of all the hazards and all the problems let us determine not only to reach this side of Jordan but to go right over to conquer and dispossess the enemy and claim our inheritance purchased for us by the blood of Christ.

I suggest that the following were some of the reasons which contributed to the failure of the people of Israel.

They easily forgot their history

Deep down in their hearts they craved for things in Egypt. They forgot how oppressive, devastating and destructive life was for them in Egypt. They forgot the clay pits, taskmasters' whips, the heavy burdens they had to bear. Strangely enough, they felt that they had *missed* so much by following Moses out of Egypt. They longed for things in Egypt that now they could not have in their new life – the food, the sights, the gods, the music, even the graves! How easy it is to forget that the things which we thought were entertainment and enjoyment became the very things that haunted, tortured and tormented us! Things that we felt were so precious had in fact become the serpents in our bosoms that turned round and stung us.

We can forget what life was really like outside of Christ, what it is really like in the world. The rat race, the pressure, tension, stress, strain, ugliness, immorality, deceit. Any follower of Christ who wants to bring along their old life, their past attitudes, desires, motives and lust will never really enjoy this new life. The two cannot mix. They are incompatible. That is why we are told to 'come out from them and be separate' (2 Corinthians 6: 17). The past can only hinder the future.

We must not allow our past to shape our future. We must have the strength and the grace that it takes to cut ourselves free from the past so that we can realise our future. We are people of destiny and if we keep living in the past we will never reach our destiny.

They took God for granted after a while

After the initial excitement, the moving out of Egypt, the crossing of the Red Sea, the defeat of Pharaoh, the water and manna, after their singing, dancing, celebration and times of rejoicing, the novelty wore off. As they settled down to everyday practicalities and the nitty-gritty of life, somehow God did not seem so present, so significant, so prominent in their thinking. God receded into the background of their consciousness. They took the daily miracles of water and manna for granted; they did not praise God as much as they did before. In the pursuits of everyday life God became distant. They lost their reverence and the sense of God's holy awesomeness.

We will never succeed if we allow God to be distant in our lives, taking him for granted. Mary and Joseph discovered that Jesus was not with them after a whole day's journey. I wonder how long you have gone in your prayer life and in your daily walk without recognising that Jesus is not there? In your church, your meetings, your activities, is Jesus there? What a tragic and moving scene to see Jesus standing outside his church and knocking at the door, seeking admission: 'Here I am! I stand at the door and knock. If anyone hears my voice and opens the door, I will go in and eat with him, and he with me' (Revelation 3: 20). Where is Jesus at this point in your life? Is he on the outside or on the inside?

After a time, the people of Israel began to treat God as part of the furniture. It is important for us always to retain in our hearts the sense of God's sovereignty and that sense of his glorious holiness and absolute majesty. Nothing should cloud our sensitivity to who God really is: almighty, God of majesty, transcendent, yet our Emmanuel. The God of glory, cradled in a manger. Incarnate Christ yet conquering Lord. Crucified lamb yet risen, resurrected. The God who is author of creation, head of the church, king of the kingdom.

They lost their implicit trust in God

They murmured and complained when they were tested and tried. Although God gave them victory over the armies of Pharaoh, parted the Red Sea and provided for their every need, they still could not trust themselves to his care. You would have thought that at the frontier of Canaan they would instinctively have turned to God in implicit trust. Yet to their shame and our warning we know that they miserably failed. They instinctively worried. Jesus said, 'Seek first God's kingdom and his righteousness, and all these things will be given to you as well' (Matthew 6: 33). Our worrying, our anxiety, our tension, stress and fretfulness do not really bring answers. They make matters worse. But our faith, placed simply in a God who is able to clothe the lillies and to provide for the sparrows, is far more effective than all our worrying. They failed because they had forgotten how to trust God. Have we? The Christian life is basically a life of faith at all levels and at all times.

They were unwilling to accept discipline

Discipline was essential for their growth and development. As we have already seen, they were willing to enjoy the blessings but rejected the discipline. God knows that there is a little rebel in each of us. Deep down in every human heart is a rebellious person. And all rebellion is basically against God. We do not like God's way because it is so much higher than our ways. We do not like what God likes, because it is so contrary to our own likes and dislikes. God tells us to love when we really want to hate, to forgive when we really want to bear a grudge. God tells us to turn the other cheek and to walk away when we really want to stand up and fight for our rights. The Lord tells us to be kind when really we'd rather not bother; to help others when really we feel we are the ones who need help; to give out of our need instead of wanting to receive.

If we will be true followers of Jesus then, like him, we need to learn how to love the unloveable and to be kind to the unkind, to help even if it means sacrifice, to be meek and lowly and humble in spirit. We are the

Lord's raw material. In order to refine us and make us into a work of art certain disciplines are necessary: the discipline of prayer and fasting, the discipline of reading the word and feeding on the word, the discipline required to get involved in the life of the community, to be committed to your husband or wife, the discipline of being a good parent, the discipline that is required to make meaningful contributions to the rest of the community of believers. It requires real discipline to be selfless, loving, generous and committed.

The Israelites did not want to do anything they did not feel like doing. They rejected anything that did not suit them or was not convenient to them. Because they rejected those disciplines they left behind them woeful tales of a lawless, troublesome, disgruntled, very awkward people who never ever fully made it into the promises of God.

They became comfortable with the desert

They grew so accustomed to the life in the desert that they became comfortable with it. They accepted the status quo. They had got used to their surroundings and their environment. They had learnt how to survive in the desert and felt secure in it. Any thought of moving on, conquering new territory or making progress would have disturbed their lifestyle. It seemed unnecessarily risky. They had lost the vision of life in the Promised Land and had settled for second best. They lacked the fire that true vision brings, the courage required to move on, the boldness required to conquer and to pioneer. They were no longer a pioneering people. They had become settlers and every bone, sinew and nerve in their bodies longed for comfort, ease and quiet. Their sense of divine mission had cooled off.

So often Christians settle for second best. We cannot stir ourselves to make the necessary sacrifices to conquer new territories for God. We have grown so accustomed to our present way of life, and so secure in what we are and what we have, that there is no deep longing and hunger in our hearts for greater, higher or better things. We have lost the art of dreaming. We need to regain it. We need to regain a vision of what our full potential in God can be, and be refired in our passion to march forward to take new territory, cross new rivers, dispossess new enemies and conquer new mountains.

They chose second best

The people of Israel flirted with their God-given destiny, always keeping half an eye on Egypt, and never fully committing themselves to the path God had mapped out for them. There is a long queue of people who were called by God to serve in specific areas but did not give that calling the priority it deserved. They could not make the sacrifices it demanded. Some have done very well at other things and, by the standards of the world, are successful but they will tell you they are haunted, unfulfilled and unhappy. They tried to short-circuit God's plan by going for easy options. They chose second best and live the rest of their lives regretting it.

They made wrong choices:

- *They chose to believe the wrong things.* Instead of relying on the promises of God they chose to question the truth and allowed the facts around them – what they could *see* – to fill them with doubts and unbelief. They doubted God's ability to deliver.

- *They chose to listen to the wrong people.* They chose to listen to the negative reports of the ten spies and to ignore the reports of Joshua and Caleb. Such negativism had a debilitating effect. When people are constantly negative and complaining, faith and trust are undermined.
- *They chose to accept wrong values.* Because they set their hearts on security, material comfort, and milking the present for all it was worth, they ended up disobeying God. If our eyes are not on him alone, our values will become distorted and we will start making distorted choices.
- *They chose to replace God with an idol.* God was no longer the object of their love and worship. They replaced God in their hearts.
- *They chose to have a wrong mentality* – a grasshopper mentality. Instead of choosing to believe that God had destined them for great things, they devalued themselves. Instead of choosing to believe God when he said how much he loved them, they chose to put themselves down. They accepted a wrong assessment of their usefulness to God.

These were not just a strange band of rabble rousers but a people chosen by God for a specific calling. God's short-term vision for them was entry and possession of the Promised Land, but he also had a long term purpose: to build them up to be his prophetic people pointing the way to Jesus through whom all the nations of the earth would be blessed. They held the destiny of the nations in their hands. But they flirted with their mission and placed it in jeopardy. Let us not flirt with God's calling and purpose for our lives but make a commitment to be true to God's will, whatever the cost.

8

BUILDING COMMUNITY

No man is an island. It is not God's intention that anyone should live in splendid isolation. God created us with the capacity for companionship. He said of Adam, 'It is not good for the man to be alone' (Genesis 2:18).

God, in his infinite wisdom, has designed the human being to live in community. It is essential for us to live as part of a community if we are to thrive and attain the purpose for which we were created.

God is a progressive God and the time had come for the children of Israel to be moulded into a community and nation. They had to move on from the spectacular deliverances and victories, to specific order. God was ready to take them further into his purposes for them. To make progress they must move from individual freedom to collective responsibility; from personal deliverances to developing relationships – relationships which would provide them with the support and strength that they needed to build their future. They needed to move from personal ambitions to corporate function, each person finding his or her rightful place and making his or her individual contribution to the building up of the whole.

To isolate ourselves from society is to deny ourselves the opportunity to enrich and enhance our lives by the variety and complementarity that others provide. Not only will we be impoverished but we will not develop properly as human beings. We will be the poorer for our isolation. It was the same for the children of Israel. In order to escape finally from the shackles of slavery, it was imperative for them to organise themselves, to function as a community and to share a corporate life. If they were to reach their destiny, the embryo of a nation which had been formed and forged in the iron furnace of Pharaoh's world, must now be strengthened and come to maturity.

COMMUNITY ORGANISED IN SMALL GROUPS

Let's look more closely at the step by step process God used in organising this great crowd of people.

Moses' father-in-law, Jethro, heard about all the amazing things God had done for the people in their exit from Egypt, and decided to come and visit him. Speaking with Moses face to face about it all, Jethro was convinced. 'Now I know that the Lord is greater than all other gods, for he did this to those who had treated Israel arrogantly', he said. Jethro then acted on that realisation and brought sacrifices to God, and his joyful conversion to the God of Abraham was celebrated with a feast. Aaron and all the elders of Israel were invited to come along to it too.

> 'The next day Moses took his seat to serve as judge for the people, and they stood around him from morning till evening. When his father-in-law saw all that Moses was doing for the people, he said, "What is this you are doing for the people? Why do you alone sit as judge, while all these people stand around your from morning till evening?"
>
> Moses answered him, "Because the people come to me to seek God's will. Whenever they have a dispute, it is brought to me, and I decide between the parties and inform them of God's decrees and laws."
>
> Moses' father-in-law replied, "What you are doing is not good. You and these people who come to you will only wear yourselves out. The work is too heavy for you; you cannot handle it alone. Listen now to me and I will give you some advice, and may God be with you. You must be the people's representative before God and bring their disputes to him. Teach them the decrees and laws, and show them the way to live and the duties they are to perform. But select capable men from all the people – men who fear God, trustworthy men who hate dishonest gain – and appoint them as officials over thousands, hundreds, fifties and tens. Have them serve as judges for the people at all times, but have them bring every difficult case to you; the simple cases they can decide themselves. That will make your load lighter, because they will share it with you. If you do this and God so commands, you will be able to stand the strain, and all these people will go home satisfied."

> Moses listened to his father-in-law and did everything he said. He chose capable men from all Israel and made them leaders of the people, officials over thousands, hundreds, fifties and tens. They served as judges for the people at all times. The difficult cases they brought to Moses, but the simple ones they decided themselves.' *Exodus 19: 13–26*

Moses was already overladen and over burdened with all the complaints and disputes among the children of Israel. A million and a half people bold enough to grumble against God, would have a lot of disputes to settle! They needed a judicial system that was practical and manageable. The one Jethro suggested would do this, but would also enable the leaders appointed to carry out effective pastoral care. People would be counselled, encouraged, helped and facilitated in their walk with God and to keep the covenant God made with them. That is why it was important for them to be organised in manageable proportions; it was vital to be both efficient and effective.

Leadership and community building

An essential ingredient in the provision of pastoral care was the appointing of quality leaders. Leaders who would not settle for mediocrity but would aim for the highest and best for God and his people. Leaders who would strive for excellence, for whom nothing but the best is good enough for their God and for his people. They had to be people who feared God, people of integrity and wisdom, who would listen to the heart cries of the people just as God had listened and heard when they cried out to him in Egypt. They had to be people who would judge righteously and impartially, free from prejudice of every kind, whether racial or linked to status. Not even the alien should be discriminated against. These leaders had to be people who would judge without fear of man, always remembering that God is the final judge.

It is important to note that this system included a higher court, a place of appeal, a person to whom they could refer the matters that they could not solve. Moses was to function in an 'apostolic' capacity in this respect. Jesus, similarly, called twelve disciples, then the seventy and later one hundred and twenty. Through their ministry to each other, he formed and moulded them into a visible community of people. On the day of Pentecost, three thousand people responded to Christ when Peter preached to them. Straight away, the twelve apostles did two significant things. One was to make sure that these new converts laid firm foundations on which they could build their Christian experiences, so they were urged to give themselves continuously to the apostle's doctrine, to prayer, to fellowship and to breaking of bread. The second thing the apostles did was to form them into a community, a community where they cared for each other and they shared with each other until no one was any longer in need (see Acts 2: 37–47).

One of the great lacks in much Christianity today is that we do not have meaningful relationships. We have churches, meetings, membership rules, sing out of the same hymn book, listen to the same preacher year in and year out, belong to the same church – but know little or nothing of each other. There is very little caring and sharing. We have not yet learnt how to weep with those who weep or to rejoice with those who rejoice, because we have not learnt the secret of building relationships. We don't put time and effort into things that will help relationships to be built. Like the children of Israel and the early church, we need to be organised, structuring ourselves in ways that will lead to the building and deepening of relationships. Smaller, more manageable groups, although still part of the whole church, need to be planned and given appropriate leadership. The major function of these groups is to provide pastoral care: to build genuine friendships, provide an environment and context that will enable the development of character and gifts, and to create a sense of identity and belonging. Leaders must be facilitators and enablers of the people of God. They must themselves be under leadership, accountable to 'apostolic' authority as these leaders were accountable to Moses.

Jesus is our final judge but he has placed leaders and pastors in the church – elders, apostles and prophets – through whom and with whom his rule and his reign would flow to his people. No one can be a *substitute* for Jesus in a believer's life, neither should there be 'heavy shepherding' or discipline that takes away the individual's choice and responsibility. However, we need to ask ourselves whether, because of inadequate structures, we are denying ourselves the means of fostering kingdom life and promoting kingdom activity among us, as God was seeking through Moses to do with the children of Israel. Basic human needs remain the same. We have the same need for love, for care, for guidance, for counselling, even to settle our disputes.

Let us put the necessary structures into place that will enable this to happen lest we be guilty of poor management and misrule. (see Isaiah 32: 1–8.)

A NEW RELATIONSHIP

> 'In the third month after the Israelites left Egypt – on the very day – they came to the Desert of Sinai. After they set out from Rephidim, they entered the Desert of Sinai, and Israel camped there in the desert in front of the mountain.' *Exodus 19: 1–2*

A new chapter was opening up in the history of God's people. Sinai was the highest peak in a range of mountains sitting right in the middle of a desolate and barren desert. It was covered with thorny bushes overlooking a plain of 400 or more acres. It was here that God commanded the children of Israel to pitch their tents for a period while he prepared them for nationhood. They were about to be initiated into a whole new dimension of life.

Moses, too, faced a change in his role. Up to this point God had used him as a prophet and deliverer; now he would take on more and more of a pastoral role but would emerge particularly as the people's law-giver and judge. His prophetic role, particularly as directed against Pharaoh, was now mostly swallowed up by his pastoral task, which was directed to the people of God.

> 'Then Moses went up to God, and the Lord called to him from the mountain and said, "This is what

> you are to say to the house of Jacob and what you are to tell the people of Israel: 'You yourselves have seen what I did to Egypt, and how I carried you on eagles' wings and brought you to myself. Now if you obey me fully and keep my covenant, then out of all nations you will be my treasured possession. Although the whole earth is mine, you will be for me a kingdom of priests and a holy nation.' These are the words you are to speak to the Israelites."
>
> So Moses went back and summoned the elders of the people and set before them all the words the Lord had commanded him to speak. The people all responded together, "We will do everything the Lord has said." So Moses brought their answer back to the Lord.' *Exodus 19: 3–8*

The transition from dramatic rescues, the miracles of provision and mighty victories, to the building up of a community, was difficult. Moulding a community was a task far more formidable than they imagined. As the man said, 'It was not easy, mate. Not easy at all!'

It is hardly surprising, really, when one considers how traumatic events had been for the Hebrew people. It must have been an awful experience to be held in captivity by Pharaoh. Unimaginable. They probably developed a lot of complexes. We can hardly blame them for being sceptical and cynical. It was probably their long years of abuse that had led them to be so fearful and why they found it difficult to trust anyone when faced with problems, even difficult to trust the Lord. No wonder Moses in turn found it such a difficult task to mould this people into a cohesive nation.

The whole point of the Exodus was to lead the people of Israel into a new and fuller life, to enjoy the richest and the best in God. This was true freedom. But God had now to teach them that human freedom cannot be separated from responsibility and privilege.

Here at Sinai the Lord reminded them that he carried them out of Egypt as an eagle would carry her young. Why? To cause them to soar as eagles themselves into the heights, far removed from all the drudgery, bondage, fear and torment of the clay pits of Egypt. He wanted them to enjoy him, as he would take pleasure in them. So he promised to make a commitment to his people, a binding agreement. He would be faithful and stand by them, and he expected a reciprocal commitment to be made by them to him. People who have been redeemed have been redeemed *to* God, and are kept in that relationship to him by his covenant with them. A covenant people demonstrate their appreciation of God by submitting to him in humble obedience and in following his instructions.

It is important that, as God's redeemed people, we should walk in obedience to him because:

- This shows that we love and appreciate him.
- People will see that we are God's special possession when they see that our lives are different.
- Our role as a prophetic witness to all peoples will only then be effective. A materialistic and secular world under the control of Satan, a world that has gone wild, lost and hopeless, where sin and evil reign, and where the existence of a God is not acknowledged, desperately needs an alternative model of living. God's kingdom people are to lighten the darkness and to demonstrate that there is hope, that there is another way to live,

there is another choice.

If Israel had caught the vision of the higher calling of God they might have been more cooperative. Had they realised the importance of their responsibility to be the vehicle to carry salvation to the nations, they might have behaved more responsibly. If they knew they were to be God's model society to demonstrate God's love they would not, I believe, have murmured, complained and rebelled as much as they did. It is important for God's people today not to lose sight, like they did, of our real purpose: to provide the world with a demonstration model of the kingdom. I long that our hearts should burn with a vision of the kingdom and a passion to free people, so that we can be channels through which his power and love can reach the victims of sin.

From the spectacular to the specific

Sinai was to prove a real turning point in the history of the people of Israel. The Lord had changed their condition of slavery and given them liberty, but here at Sinai he gave them what is referred to as the Decalogue, Ten Commandments or the Law. It was a new constitution to bring them under his government. Also here at Sinai the Lord gave them instructions to erect the tabernacle. The Law and the tabernacle would alter and regulate their concept of worship, fellowship with God and relationship with each other.

> 'On the morning of the third day there was thunder and lightning, with a thick cloud over the mountain, and a very loud trumpet blast. Everyone in the camp

> trembled. Then Moses led the people out of the camp to meet with God, and they stood at the foot of the mountain. Mount Sinai was covered with smoke, because the Lord descended on it in fire. The smoke billowed up from it like smoke from a furnace, the whole mountain trembled violently, and the sound of the trumpet grew louder and louder. Then Moses spoke and the voice of God answered him.' *Exodus 19: 16–19*

At Sinai, the people not only witnessed spectacular wonders and miracles but, as a prelude to the new phase in their development, it was necessary for them to have a new meeting with God. The future must be built on a fresh revelation of God. It was an august and solemn occasion, a frightening and awesome experience. Before they could proceed with anything further it was vital that they should hear God. At Sinai Israel entered one of the most influential epochs of their history, a period that would have national and international impact and would have lasting effect on many generations. The world has never been the same since!

Moses was only a type, a forerunner, a prophecy to the whole of humanity. His whole life was an expression of things in the heart of God for all people everywhere. God looked down through the corridors of time and he saw multitudes, humanity held in the bondage of sin, under the tyranny and domination of Satan's evil powers, and he determined to send a saviour and deliverer greater than Moses to rescue them from their chains. God saw a world filled with corruption and darkness, needing a light and a model. It needed an alternative that was authentic, a demonstration model to show what life can be like when people submit themselves to the government of God. He saw our world in chaos and confusion, needing God's order. He saw the hatred, bloodshed and divisions among people, who needed to live in harmony. And so God sent Jesus, One greater than Moses. The law-giver at Sinai now invites us to seek his kingdom rule and righteousness in Jesus. For the Kingdom of God is here now because Jesus is here. Whenever people open up their lives and submit to his lordship he will give them rest. As God did with Israel at Sinai, he will build all who come to him through Christ into a community that will be a model for the whole world and a vehicle to fulfil his kingdom purposes here on earth.

COMMUNITY BUILT ON SOLID FOUNDATIONS

Such a society must be built on sound kingdom principles: equality and justice. 'For the kingdom of God is not a matter of eating and drinking, but righteousness, peace and joy in the Holy Spirit' (Romans 14:17). These foundations can be designed and built only by God himself. This is also why Jesus said to us that our lives should be built on the rock. Paul said, 'No-one can lay any foundation other than the one already laid, which is Jesus Christ' (1 Corinthians 3: 11). We need to be built on the solid rock. At Sinai God was laying the foundations which would guide the people of Israel through life by means of the Law. These were words which came from the throne of God, words of life and words for living.

The principles on which their lives were built and governed fall into two main categories. Firstly, principles which govern their relationship with God; secondly, principles which govern their relationship with their fellow men. Relationship is what the Christian life is all about. When the Lord Jesus was asked what is the greatest commandment he replied, ' "Love the Lord your God with all your heart and with all your soul and with all your mind." This is the first and greatest commandment. The second is like it: "Love your neighbour as yourself." All the Law and the Prophets hang on these two commandments.' (Matthew 22:37–40.) This was a direct reference to the things that God delivered to Moses for Israel at Mount Sinai.

If we will follow the Lord and fulfill his Kingdom purposes we, too, must learn how to move from our freedom to be formed into a community. We must build our lives on solid foundations. Our whole experience must be built on a strong and loving relationship with God and also with our fellow men. This is not a popular philosophy in our time because we live in such a materialistic world where consumerism is the order of the day. It is not convenient for us to build and maintain strong relationships with other people. In the pursuit to get on in life, to succeed, to make it, we can end up trampling others under our feet to get what we want. In our struggle we cannot spend the time and energy that is necessary to have quality relationships with other people. We just can't afford it! Yet if we are to be the followers of Christ we have no option. We are not simply given a ticket to glory land. We are not only forgiven and washed from our sins but we are also meant to use our new-found freedom, our new-found life, to demonstrate the Kingdom to the world, to be a model.

9

PRINCIPLES FOR LIVING

'And God spoke all these words' (Exodus 20:1). The Lord gave the new nation, Israel, a constitution for living. It was essential for them to be structured but also to be instructed in the ways of God. Structure without life is a skeleton. Life without structure is a heap of confusion. Ten commandments and other detailed instructions were given as guidelines for religious, social and civil affairs. These were not to form the ground for their salvation, but were to be a guide for how they should live as saved people. The Law could never bring people to salvation, because none of us is capable of keeping it all. Rather, now that the people were freed and saved they needed to order their lives to fit in with the expressed will of God.

PRINCIPLES FOR LIVING

To please God must always remain our highest motive. Even Jesus said, 'I always do what pleases him' (John 8:29), and if we will please God then we need to surrender ourselves totally to his will, for to love God is to do his will. 'If you love me,' Jesus said, 'you will obey what I command' (John 14:15).

Before God gave the people these commands he called them to consecrate themselves and to renew their covenant with him. The maintenance of their covenant was so essential to their success. Conduct flows out of consecration. Doing results from being. To live God's way we need to have God's life. It is easy to lapse into the frame of mind that takes advantage of the grace of God by ignoring the scriptural principles and doing our own thing, without checking to see if what we do lines up with what God wants. Our life and conduct, our value systems, should be shaped and governed by God's principles for living. Christianity is distinctive among all other religions because it alone marries doctrine with ethics, belief with behaviour, conviction with conduct, faith with works, attitude with action, principles with practice. Anything else is inconsistent. Jesus called it hypocrisy. This is the reason why God carefully gave such elaborate and detailed instructions to Israel, to pattern and build the new nation on sound practices reflecting God's own heart.

Too often, we neglect this most significant aspect of Christian living. As a result, we are inconsistent. A great gap exists between the things we say and believe and the things we do. Our prophetic function and witness to the world is reduced and loses its potency because of this inconsistency. Our impact on the world for God and good is reduced almost to a zero. People treat us as irrelevant and insignificant, with little or nothing to offer them. We who were meant to be the salt and light of society are now seen as humbugs. We who were meant to give leadership and pave the way for others to follow are ourselves being led by the godless philosophies of our time. We are enmeshed in the unjust, ungodly system of this world and haven't the good sense to be distinct and separate! Once this has happened we forfeit our right to be a voice for God. In the midst of a crooked and perverse generation the Lord is still longing for a people of integrity – a chosen, priestly, holy nation – to rise up, shine, and proclaim the greatness and love of God.

There is a tendency to make a distinction between the ten commandments and the other instructions given in the subsequent chapters of Exodus (chapters 21–24). It is better to treat them all as one. The instructions that follow were explanation and commentary on the ten, finer details of what God meant, the practical outworking of the ten. These instructions were far reaching and covered many aspects of the people's life – moral, social and civil. There are principles governing masters and servants, work ethics, physical injuries, property rights, various evil practices, their religious life, and their personal and national relationships.

A detailed study of these shows that God left nothing to their imagination! A people held in slavery and bondage for so long could be forgiven if they had lost the sense of proper values. God did not leave them to their own wisdom to formulate their own value system based on a mixture of their experiences in Egypt and the philosophies prevalent at that time to which they were exposed. We run the great danger today of interpreting the scriptures through cultural spectacles instead of allowing the scripture to interpret our culture. Sometimes we conveniently choose to understand the scripture by the philosophies of our time. Simply put, we make the scripture say what we want it to say instead of allowing the scripture to tell us what we should think and be.

God does not leave us to decide how we must live in order to please him. He tells us. He is a holy God and calls us to obey him in every detail just as he called the Israelites to obey.

COMMUNITY BUILT ON RELATIONSHIP WITH GOD

> 'And God spoke all these words:
>
> "I am the Lord your God, who brought you out of Egypt, out of the land of slavery.
>
> You shall have no other gods before me.
>
> You shall not make for yourself an idol in the form of anything in heaven above or on the earth beneath or in the waters below. You shall not bow down to them or worship them; for I, the Lord your God, am a jealous God, punishing the children for the sin of the fathers to the third and fourth generation of those who hate me, but showing love to thousands who love me and keep my commandments.
>
> You shall not misuse the name of the Lord your God, for the Lord will not hold anyone guiltless who misuses his name.
>
> Remember the Sabbath day by keeping it holy. Six days you shall labour and do all your work, but the

> seventh day is a Sabbath to the Lord your God. On it you shall not do any work, neither you, nor your son or daughter, nor your manservant or maidservant, nor your animals, nor the alien within your gates. For in six days the Lord made the heavens and the earth, the sea, and all that is in them but he rested on the seventh day. Therefore the Lord blessed the Sabbath day and made it holy." '
>
> *Exodus 20:1–12*

Let us examine more closely those principles which govern our relationship with God. There are six major points of emphasis.

1 God is pre-eminent

We should give God pre-eminence in all things in our lives. There should be no other gods, no one else who challenges God's place. He is a jealous God. He alone should be crowned as Lord to rule and govern. All the controls should be in his hands. He should have priority, the only one to whom we give our heart's worship.

2 No idolatry

No kind of idolatry was permitted. In our time we may scoff at the idea that idolatry exists because we are so sophisticated. Think again! Idolatry is simply anything or anyone who comes before God in our lives. Just as the Israelites were prohibited to have idols, so are we. Anyone or anything which comes before Jesus in our lives challenges our allegiance to him. God is the only one worthy to have our unquestioned allegiance.

3 Worship is central

There were principles which governed worship. Worship is the lovely and wonderful privilege that we are given to come into his presence, to pour out our love and our adoration in praises and thanksgiving. Worship was to be central in the life of the people of God; its centrality highlighted by God's command to position the tabernacle centrally in the camp.

4 Day of rest

There were principles to instruct them to observe strictly a day of rest. They were encouraged to enjoy God by taking time to refresh and recreate themselves. God does not want us to endure him but to enjoy him, not to be filled with activity only, but to know him, his rest and his peace. We can be so busy with the work of the Lord that we have no time for the Lord of the work.

5 God's name is holy

There were principles which clearly warned against using the name of the Lord in vain. We are to walk in a way that is worthy of our calling. Nothing in our life should bring disrepute or reproach to the name of God. Our words, as well as our characters, should be a commendation to the one whose name we bear.

6 Worship is pure

In direct contrast to heathen practices, ceremonies and rituals, the Israelites' worship was to be pure, uncluttered, simple and sincere. Their whole life was to be built around their worship of God as their creator, redeemer and King. Love God, fear God, reverence God, for he is holy.

Our relationship with God must be based primarily on love. A love relationship is what walking with God is all about. He alone has the first and last word in all we think, say or do. To him alone we give our allegiance, worship and trust. No one else. His demands are absolute and exclusive. He demands our *all*.

COMMUNITY BUILT ON RELATIONSHIP WITH OTHERS

> ' "Honour your father and your mother, so that you may live long in the land the Lord your God is giving you.
> You shall not murder.
> You shall not commit adultery." '
>
> *Exodus 20:12–14*

There are four major points of emphasis in these commands.

Family

It is not without significance that this section of God's instruction to Israel began with the family. All relationships with one another grow out of our family relationships. Healthy families produce healthy individuals; healthy individuals produce healthy nations and communities. The home and family is the God-ordained place for people to grow and develop. It is in the family that love, care, honour, respect, trust and loyalty can flourish. Where these qualities are present they provide the right environment for proper growth and development, emotionally, psychologically and spiritually. The family is where people will find their identity and sense of belonging. It is where they should feel safe and secure. It is in the climate of a home where love and harmony exist, that people grow to be stable, develop sound values, and learn the necessary disciplines and respect so vital to encourage nobility of spirit and integrity of heart.

Where these are missing the character will be vulnerable and open for the enemy to sow evil seeds out of which evil deeds grow. It is only in a caring family context that the pain of rejection can be avoided because here each individual is accepted and valued in their own uniqueness. As parents accept responsibility to care for their children so children must accept responsibility to care for the well being of their parents. Unfortunately, modern society has encouraged our selfishness to the point where we have become so independent that we abandon our responsibility to others. State institutions cannot give the love, compassion, warmth and confidence that God intended to come from one's own immediate family. While such institutions are indeed needed and welcome they are no real substitute. Any law, institution, government or philosophy which contributes to the destruction of the home and dissolution of the family is evil. It is wicked in the extreme because hurt, loneliness, pain, emotional damage, spiritual bankruptcy and moral decadence are the inevitable consequences. In our society they are proving to be irreparable despite the gigantic efforts made by many to prevent them. To learn respect for parents is training in how to respond to and respect other authority in society. To give respect is to receive respect. To learn how to honour and appreciate your immediate family is to cultivate an attitude that appreciates others, not one that thinks only of itself. To submit to parents cuts to the root of rebellion.

It is suggested that at the beginning of the next century:

- Less than fifty percent of children in Britain will be living with both parents in conventional families.
- Up to twenty-five percent of children will have divorced parents. Others will have cohabiting parents who have split up. A total of ten percent of couples who married in 1951 had divorced by their twenty-fifth anniversary, but of those who married in 1981, ten percent were divorced after only four and a half years.
- That more children will be born outside marriage than to married mothers.
- That only seven or eight out of ten people will get married. In 1971, eighty-four percent of men and ninety-three percent of women were married by the age of thirty, but by 1987 that had fallen to fifty-seven percent for men and sixty-eight percent for women.
- That the number of cohabiting couples who presently marry after having children will decline and that the number of cohabiting couples with or without children will increase.

The same report is doubtful of the stability of the family and appears to have recognised that 'conventional family life' – that is, parents married at the time a child is born and staying together until the child is grown up – may no longer be the norm for the majority of people in Britain. However, not all changes are connected purely to an increased secularisation. The report is keen to point out that:

> 'We should recognise that some changes in British family life are closely linked to problems of poverty, unemployment and homelessness. These changes present major challenges for policy, especially in the areas of employment, social security, housing, health, education and community care. Such challenges are not being addressed at the moment. They need to be.' (*Family Change and Future Policy*, FPSC, June 1990. Joseph Rowntree Memorial Trust)

There is no higher wisdom than that of the God who created us. His order is always best. Anything else is based on self-gratification, abdication of responsibility and a callous disregard for the quality of life as God intended it. We do well to return to God's way even if it means undoing and unlearning some things. The destruction of the family and the home marks the beginning of the end of all that is good and wholesome in society.

Marriage and sexual morality

'You shall not commit adultery.' This command was meant not only in a specific and particular sense to preserve the purity and sanctity of marriage but also in a much wider sense, to instruct us in matters relating to sexual morality. The expanded version that Jesus gave of this command gives clearer insight to the heart of God. Jesus says to us, 'You have heard that it was said, "Do not commit adultery." But I tell you that anyone who looks at a woman lustfully has already committed adultery with her in his heart' (Matthew 5:27–28). Paul in his New Testament writings also makes it abundantly clear that sex outside marriage is sin. It defiles the body as a temple of the Holy Spirit:

> 'Do you not know that your bodies are members of Christ himself? Shall I then take the members of Christ and unite them with a prostitute? Never! Do you not know that he who unites himself with a prostitute is one with her in body? For it is said, "The two will become one flesh." But he who unites himself with the Lord is one with him in spirit.
>
> Flee from sexual immorality. All other sins a man commits are outside his body, but he who sins sexually sins against his own body. Do you not know that your body is a temple of the Holy Spirit, who is in you, whom you have received from God? You are not your own; you were bought at a price. Therefore honour God with your body.'
>
> *1 Corinthians 6:15–20*

In the formation of this new nation the Lord wanted to impress on the people's hearts that he wanted to live among them. But God, who is holy, cannot fill his people with his presence and dwell among them unless they are clean, including sexually clean. The Lord does not forbid sex. He created people with a sex drive but he intended that the enjoyment and pleasure derived from sex should be within the boundaries of marriage, where faithfulness and commitment between two partners were the foundation stones.

That is the reason why the Lord Jesus himself takes up the theme and Paul emphasised it so strongly. He counsels Timothy, his young protegé, to 'flee the evil desires of youth, and pursue righteousness, faith, love and peace along with those who call on the Lord out of a pure heart' (2 Timothy 2:22). In other words, do not become a slave and victim of your passions, but bring them under the government of God.

We live in a secular society where we have witnessed a great change in moral standards. The norms which were once accepted in society are now flung away. Caution is thrown to the wind. Morality that was built upon biblical foundations is now frowned upon and considered to be old-fashioned, out-dated and puritanical. Premarital sex is no longer called fornication. Fornication and immorality are looked upon as dirty words these days. Unpleasant though it is to the ear, in God's sight they are sin. What sexual immorality really means is pursuing sex for self gratification with no sense of responsibility. Outside the confines of marriage there is no long-term commitment. It is all a matter of satisfying our animal pleasure. One big experiment. Fun, with no regard to the pain, psychological and emotional damage we cause.

The practice is so common that it has become the norm of society and anyone who dares to believe otherwise is a prude and must be abnormal. The philosophy which now prevails is, 'if it feels good, do it.' Once you feel like it no one should tell you it is wrong. Not even God. We have become our own gods. We make our own rules. We serve ourselves. Anything goes, even homosexual and lesbian relationships. Degenerated and depraved minds have rationalised incestuous relationships too. Sexual abuse of children is so common that almost daily the media informs us about young children abused by grown men. People have lost all sense of decency and propriety when all kinds of perversion are now considered acceptable and normal.

God sees such things as perverse, harmful and sinful. Yet those who practice them consider it their right to do as they please. The fact that people get hurt, emotionally destroyed and spoilt for life as a result, is no concern of theirs. I am afraid God has other ideas and whether they believe in him or not a day of reckoning is coming when an account must be given. I sincerely hope they will be prepared to answer God. None of the arguments put forward for the permissiveness in our society will stand on that day.

God made sure that the emerging Israelite nation understood that immorality destroys quality of life, *especially* that of those who indulge in it. But there is good news. If you are caught in situations of sexual immorality, however involved, deeply soiled, addicted or bound you may feel, the God of love invites you to come to him. He longs to give you freedom and cleansing and is willing to intervene and give you the help you need to reconstruct your life and ensure your future happiness.

Sexual morality is a must for a society to be healthy and happy. The heavy emphasis the Lord puts on it should be enough to convince us that society must be built on sexual morality and the sanctity of marriage. We die from within otherwise.

Equality of the sexes

Closely linked with the command against sexual immorality is the teaching given later on in Exodus (see, for example 21:7–11, 22–25; 22:16–17, 22–24) that women were as precious and valuable to God as men were. So he gave the people instructions to protect the liberty and rights of women, so preserving their humanity and dignity. God is not chauvinistic, unlike the men of ancient times who showed utter disregard for the status of women, often treating them with gross contempt. The heart of God is made very explicit here. Women were not to be treated cheaply. Unlike the custom of the nations around, women were never to be treated as part of anybody's property. They were always to be treated with the decency and proper respect that they deserve as persons created in the very image and likeness of God.

Several things followed. Women were to have a right to their freedom and should never be treated unjustly. They had a right to be treated with equality. They had rights of inheritance. Laws were given to protect them from the abuse, exploitation and misuse of others. Their physical and economic weakness should not be taken advantage of. The heart of God for women is the same as it is for men. He does not treat them as second-class citizens but gives them equal place, for he created them and redeemed them, and there is no difference between male and female in the Kingdom (see Galatians 3:28).

The sanctity of human life

As God continued to restructure Israel into a society

worthy to bear his name, he left them in no doubt as to how he regards human life. He places a very high value on it. So high a value that he was willing to give his only Son to die in the place of human beings, to redeem them from the curse of death, to restore all humankind to equality and to return all people to a life in keeping with his original intention.

Murder, for whatever reason, is wrong and must be condemned. Under no circumstance can it be condoned. Throughout the ages man has shed the blood of his fellow man. It seems as though the curse has followed us since the time of Cain when he killed his brother, Abel, because of his jealousy and intense anger. We never seem to learn.

In our modern, enlightened, so-called sophisticated age we slaughter one another in ways more than one. The earth is soaked with the blood of men and women killed in umpteen wars. We have become so desensitised that we can take the lives of innocent children even before they are born, as though the unborn child has no rights at all. This we do by the million without batting an eyelid. Between March 1989 and February 1990 over 180,000 babies were aborted in England and Wales alone. How callous we can get! And we pass it off as being intelligent. Does murder become less horrible because it is devised by brilliant brains to disguise the actual atrociousness of the crime? The holocaust, Northern Ireland, South Africa, Vietnam, the Middle East – the list can go on and on. Almost every corner of the globe is filled with horror stories as massacre after massacre is committed. At the time the world is shocked, but we soon forget until the next horrible crime against humanity is committed.

James explains the source from which murder really comes. 'What causes fights and quarrels among you? Don't they come from your desires that battle within you? You want something but don't get it. You kill and covet, but you cannot have what you want. You quarrel and fight' (James 4:1–2). The grass looks greener on the other side. But if some person is standing in my way, inconveniently blocking my path to what I think will be a nicer, fuller, richer life, my thoughts may turn to murder.

Jesus, teaching his disciples on the Mount of Olives, explained to them the deeper meaning of this command, 'You shall not murder.' He explains, 'You have heard that it was said to the people long ago, "Do not murder" . . . But I tell you that anyone who is angry with his brother will be subject to judgment . . . Anyone who says, "You fool!" will be in danger of the fire of hell' (Matthew 5:21–22). God looks further than the act itself. He discerns and judges the attitude of the heart. If anger, envy, jealousy or hatred are found hidden even in the deep recesses of our hearts and mind, as far as God is concerned we stand guilty already. We need to be forgiven and cleansed from them. The attitude of heart is what really matters even if we do not lift a finger against anyone.

God therefore instructed the new nation of Israel to respect the sanctity of human life. They could not build a strong, healthy, harmonious community, and be a witness to the nations around, if their practices were no different from those of the other nations. It is known that these did not place a very high value on the lives of human beings. They lived more according to the idea of the 'survival of the fittest'. God required his people to live with each other at a much higher level than that which they had seen under Pharaoh in Egypt.

We would do well to examine our own attitudes in regard to human life. Nothing we do should bring grief, sorrow or distress to others. *Anything* that degrades or deprives any person of the full and rich quality of life which God intended for him or her to enjoy, is condemned by this commandment. Those who take away the fulness of life from others will be held responsible. Jesus said, 'Love one another as I have loved you' (John 13:24). Be it far from our hearts to kill and to hate. Instead, let us recognise how immensely valuable other people are to God, and contribute positively to each other's dignity and good.

COMMUNITY BUILT ON PERSONAL RIGHTS

> ' "You shall not steal.
> You shall not give false testimony against your neighbour.
> You shall not covet your neighbour's house. You shall not covet your neighbour's wife, or his manservant or maidservant, his ox or donkey, or anything that belongs to your neighbour." '
>
> *Exodus 20:15–17*

Private property

Although this new nation was to be a cohesive community of people, caring for and sharing with one another, it did not abrogate the right of individuals and families to own their own property. Private ownership of property and household goods is not a crime against community life provided we recognise that all we are and have belongs to the Lord and we are only made stewards of all that God has placed in our care. It is important that we hold the things given into our care lightly and do not allow earthly possessions to become the sole pursuit and preoccupation of our lives.

James gave a timely warning to all who fail in their responsibility to steward properly the things committed into their charge for the common good of all. Whatever our material blessings, we should take care not to hoard them selfishly but should cheerfully, willingly and generously give to others, especially those who are in most need.

If we read the mind of the Lord correctly here it would seem that, when this is done in the right spirit, there need be no conflict between what seem to be the apparently opposing principles of community sharing and private ownership. The problem is caused when one feeds off the other or rides on the back of the other. Greed sometimes drives people to exploit the weak and steal from the poor. Conversely, the poor throw away their dignity to steal from the rich. What is worse, covetousness can eat away in the hearts of people regardless of what they possess or do not possess. People in God's new communities are neither to steal nor covet what belongs to their neighbour but should look after their neighbour's goods as though they were their very own. Principles of honesty and integrity are essential for any group of people if they will live together in peace.

Justice

God is a God of justice. The commands and their fuller explanations tackle the thorny question of justice in society. God's people must deal justly one with another. Egypt had dealt very unjustly with them but they must be different. In the world from which they came, might was right and the strong lorded it over the weak. They were to live under a very different system, so the Lord outlined to them, in detail, how to make amicable and appropriate restitution where loss or damage is done to anyone's person or property. Justice must be done to the satisfaction of all concerned.

Some of the terms used in the detailed 'case studies' of Exodus 22:1–14 seem crude and 'over the top'. But we must consider them in the context of their time. We have no excuse not to embrace their basic lessons: justice and equality of rights are to be accorded to each individual whatever his or her social status. These commands teach us to respect the rights of individuals, their person and private property. The commands not to steal, lie, or covet were directed at the deep, hidden motives of the heart. They addressed the attitudes of dishonesty and envy. Along with covetousness and greed, these attitudes lie at the very heart of injustice. Adam and Eve erred simply because they wanted that which God had forbidden. It was not God's will for them. Paul said, 'The love of money is the root of all evil.' Simple, yet so profound, and people everywhere fall into this trap. They desire to have what is not rightfully theirs to have.

Honesty

You will agree that the lessons God sought to teach the children of Israel and the foundations he tried to lay in their society are guidelines applicable even for us today. The same problems and issues which faced them in those days have not gone away. Cheating, lying, stealing and covetousness exist in our society, as do rising crime rates, muggings, thefts, injustices and corruption at all levels. Even in the most unsuspected quarters, where people do not have the need to steal or lie, people can be so gripped by greed that they become dishonest and defraud and deprive others.

God desired his people to be characterised by integrity, honesty and trust, a society where people do not seek to score points off one another. A society that is free from people who put one another down, seek to reach the top of the ladder by climbing over others, who spread rumours to bring about another's downfall. Instead, it was to be a society of individuals who would seek to build up, encourage and promote the good and the welfare of others. God wanted a society where relationships were based on truth and reality not religiosity.

These principles are applicable in our time. We should aim to walk in the light with each other, caring for one another. Let us dare to be a people worthy to bear the name of the Lord Jesus. We may have to change some of our concepts and agendas in order to do so and turn around our activities in order to make corporate life a real possibility.

10

A GOD WHO CARES

God expressed his concern for the poor, disadvantaged and underprivileged very strongly to Moses and the Israelites. As we have seen, when the children of Israel were in Egypt they suffered greatly under their task masters. They were given no status and were counted as people without any real value. But now that the Lord was forging them into a new people, he was giving them very different standards to live by:

> ' "These are the laws you are to set before them:
>
> If you buy a Hebrew servant, he is to serve you for six years. But in the seventh year, he shall go free, without paying anything. If he comes alone, he is to go free alone; but if he has a wife when he comes, she is to go with him. If his master gives him a wife and she bears him sons or daughters, the woman and her children shall belong to her master, and only the man shall go free.

> But if the servant declares, 'I love my master and my wife and children and do not want to go free,' then his master must take him before the judges. He shall take him to the door or the door-post and pierce his ear with an awl. Then he will be his servant for life.
>
> If a man sells his daughter as a servant, she is not to go free as men-servants do. If she does not please the master who has selected her for himself, he must let her be redeemed. He has no right to sell her to foreigners, because he has broken faith with her. If he selects her for his son, he must grant her the rights of a daughter. If he marries another woman, he must not deprive the first one of her food, clothing and marital rights. If he does not provide her with these three things, she is to go free, without any payment of money." ' *Exodus 21:1–11*

One is left in no doubt as to how God feels about the poor in society. These decrees are not optional but are statutory, mandatory injunctions. Imperatives. God has a bias towards the weak, helpless and powerless who are completely at the mercy of the rich and powerful. The Israelites could fully identify with this situation, given their own experiences in Egypt. Knowing what is in the heart of people everywhere, however, the Lord laid down specific moral precepts, maxims for society which are more than good advice – decrees of the King. The Lord of heaven and earth cares for the despised and down-trodden of our world.

RELEASE PEOPLE!

The Lord instructed the children of Israel to have a sabbatical year when slaves were to be set free, returned to their original status and given the rights belonging to all free men. By this practice they would no longer be obliged to serve other men except by their own choice. This, however, did not place them above the law. They, like all other people, must also respect law, which was designed for the progress, protection and common good of all. Those who had been oppressed in Egypt were not now to become oppressors. There was one law for all, irrespective of status or position. The same rights were given to the weak, helpless, slaves, orphans, widows, foreigners, homeless, unemployed and disadvantaged.

There are several words in Exodus chapters 21 to 23 that emphatically demonstrate God's loving care and involvement with ordinary people. God was not ashamed to be identified with the slaves, underprivileged children, disadvantaged neighbours, defenceless women, victims of various crimes and sufferers of injustice. When he speaks to the Israelites he uses words such as:

- *Freedom:* 'In the seventh year he shall go free' (Exodus 21: 1).
- *Rights:* 'He must not deprive the first one of her food, clothing and marital rights' (Exodus 21: 10).
- *Redemption:* 'He must let her be redeemed' (Exodus 21: 8).
- *Restitution:* 'A thief must certainly make restitution.' If a man's livestock stray 'and graze in another man's

field, he must make restitution from the best of his own field or vineyard' (Exodus 22: 3, 5).

- *Justice:* 'Do not pervert justice by siding with the crowd, and do not show favouritism to a poor man in his lawsuit . . . Do not deny justice to your poor people in the lawsuits' (Exodus 23: 2, 6).

The Lord was very careful to stress the value and importance he placed on people who in the eyes of the world may be considered insignificant, and whose rights may be trampled under the feet of those who are more powerful and privileged. No one is a forgotten person as far as God is concerned. He whose eyes are on the sparrow also watches over you. His heart for the unfortunate and unprotected comes through again and again. He made sure that all Israel knew whose side he was on. He protects the right of the poor, he hears their cries for help, he defends their cause, he fights their battles, he is angry against their oppressors, he prescribes appropriate penalties and compensation for crimes committed against them, for any damage, injury or loss sustained to their person or property. He decrees measures for the freedom of those whose misfortune and poverty place them under obligation. He condemns injustice and exploitation.

The heart of God is the same for all people in all ages. They are entitled to their freedom, their service must be justly rewarded. They must be treated with respect and given their dignity and nothing should be done to reduce their value and humanity. They should have the right to exercise free will, the right to redemption whatever their status, they should always be protected from the treacherous dealings and exploitation of unscrupulous and wicked people. The rights of women must be enshrined for they are equals with men and should be treated with dignity.

SPIRITUAL AND PRACTICAL GO TOGETHER

The laws God gave to Israel are both judicial and spiritual in nature. They constituted a national legal system, based on a framework of basic ethical norms. They also formed a value system on which their spiritual lives were built and out of which their spirituality should flow. These laws were not intended to be restrictive but to widen the people's horizons, stimulate their vision, enable them to cultivate godly attitudes and develop a positive lifestyle. God was showing them a higher way to live. They constitute a call to leave our past behind us and, in so doing, never to compromise God's standards or borrow from other religions, world views or philosophies. God has a unique purpose for his people.

Other religions and systems separate the civil, legal, moral and religious aspects of our lives. They divide up our lives into different portions, departmentalising us in order to analyse and control us. But God sees us as we are. All our life is one life; secular and spiritual are inseparable. Made in the image of God, we possess that rare quality of unity that belongs to God. We were never intended to be schizophrenic but to live in peace and harmony with ourselves. Behaviour flows from belief, works from faith, conduct from conviction, deeds from doctrines, practice from principles.

PRINCIPLES FOR ALL TIME

You may well think that all these laws are irrelevant to us as we enter the twenty-first century. You may even argue that we have progressed far beyond all the cruelty and primitive behaviour of Pharaoh's time. Unfortunately, though the circumstances may be different, the principle that works in the heart of man to oppress and exploit his fellow man is still very much alive. The strong still overpower the weak, the rich enslave the poor and the defenseless are imprisoned and made to serve the mighty.

It is not easy to define poverty because it is a relative thing. One man's poverty is another man's wealth. The inability to provide the basic needs for oneself and family is a good way by which to judge or measure poverty. An organisation working among the poor in this country says, 'anyone living on supplementary benefit must be considered to be a poor person, anyone living below the poverty line.' It must, however, be said that the Bible does not tolerate the idle poor or the idle rich in any shape or form. Scripture does not endorse lack of initiative and industry. Laziness is not countenanced.

But a poor person can also be described as anyone who is robbed of his or her sense of value, self-esteem, human rights or dignity. For whatever reason, even though he is rich in earthly possessions someone may be poor in other respects. There are many poor people who have earthly goods yet suffer the poverty of loneliness. They lead bankrupt lives, empty of meaning. Their lives lack content, quality, eternal substance.

Yet the more obvious poverty remains. Poor people

are those caught in the debt trap, who see no hope and no way out. The poor are those who have been rendered powerless and made hopeless and helpless; destitute with no future, no light at the end of their tunnel.

Our world has many overcrowded cities where poverty reigns unchecked. Millions starve. Thirty percent of us live in affluence and luxury while the other seventy percent scrape the bottom of the barrel. They barely survive. There is a growing underclass even in some of the more affluent countries of our world. In spite of all the advances in modern technology there are still millions who go to bed every night without a proper meal. Prisons around the world are filled with those whose human rights have been violated, people who are persecuted for their political and religious convictions. It is estimated that fifty-one percent of the world's population will be living in overcrowded cities by the year 2000. No wonder one commentator remarked, 'Earth is fast becoming a planet of slums.' 433 cities have a population of over one million. Seventy-nine cities have over four million citizens. Seven cities have a population of over ten·million and three cities have a population of over twenty million.

Each city is a world in miniature. In many cases they are a conglomeration of races, cultures and religions. Negative elements such as drugs, crime and poverty flourish within their confines. In every city two worlds exist side by side, one world of prosperity where the middle and upper classes flourish. The other is one of extreme poverty and hardship. The plight of the homeless and the many thousands who live below the poverty line is fast approaching gigantic proportions and is proving an embarrassment to many governments.

A survey carried out by the Food and Agriculture Organisation of the United Nations shows that at least 460 million people are suffering today from protein-energy malnutrition. And this is in a world where some countries complain of tremendous food mountains which have become a burden to them. Half of the world's population, nearly 300 million, are badly undernourished. The callousness and apathy with which we treat the handicapped, the lonely and elderly in our midst is an indictment against us and an insult to our humanity. Isn't it a travesty of justice that we are willing to spend enormous sums on weapons of destruction but find all manner of excuses and scruples to prevent us from releasing finances for the development of the poor and the needy?

One may think that the days of slavery are over but it is a scandal to witness how unashamedly and blatantly the poorer nations continue to be exploited, without any recourse to justice. The enormous debt problems that the so-called donor nations impose on the poorer nations are like millstones hanging about their necks, a burden from which they can never recover. This is not to excuse the mismanagement, corruption and oppression which takes place within those nations themselves. It is the story of Pharaoh all over again, man oppressing his fellow man, inflicting tremendous burdens and afflicting them with hard labour. We are not yet free. We need to hear the heart of God again for the peoples of the world. God says, do not illtreat the weak and the poor among you.

AN EXPANDING UNDERCLASS

An expanding underclass? Where? In the UK and Europe. 'No! Impossible', I hear you say. But the facts speak so clearly that one is left almost speechless. We try to ignore the fact that Britain is a classist society, although we recognise that there is an élite, a middle and a working class. But an underclass? Never.

In 1989, the *Independent* ran an article explaining the growth of this phenomenon in Britain. It is characterised by increases in illegitimacy, violent crime and drop-out rates from schools and the labour force. There is a dramatic increase in children born to unmarried mothers in low income sections of the community. In some inner city areas these account for as many as forty-six percent of the births. This is not a problem caused by or peculiar to the black communities in the UK, as common myths would have us believe. It is suggested that the figure would only drop by one percent if there were no blacks at all in Britain. As a matter of fact, the general illegitimacy percentage is reduced when the ethnic minorities such as Chinese, East Africans, Asians, Arabs, Indians, Pakistanis, are *included*. The point is that illegitimacy, poverty and crime rates cannot be dismissed as a 'minority' problem. Neither can the moral deterioration and decline in family cohesiveness be blamed on the influx of immigrants.

There is a general feeling among young adults and teenagers in the underclass that it does not pay to work. They see no reason to when they can survive on a welfare state. They do not see that work has any moral value attached to it; it is merely one way to make money. As a result of this prevailing attitude we produce more and more unskilled people unfit to compete in the open job market. It is an attitude problem, not merely an economic one.

All the government programmes, inner city development projects, youth training schemes and social engineering, while providing some temporary relief here and there, cannot cure the underlying causes of poverty and broken relationships. People's attitudes need to be changed. There is a need to correct injustices where they exist, to increase opportunities for education and jobs, but until the hearts of people are changed there is little hope. We can pour in millions of pounds, and some situations will undoubtedly improve, but I doubt that the real quality of life will be affected to any great degree.

It is the prophetic purpose and mission of the church to make the difference.

* * *

One rainy night Muriel opened our front door to the ring of the bell to find two tired, distressed young men standing there with two travel bags. 'Is this the pastor's house?' the older one asked. 'Yes,' she replied as politely as she could, but could not disguise her perplexity. We had never seen them before. 'Come in,' she said as invitingly as she could under the circumstances. Later, as we sat down over a cup of tea, they told us how they had to leave home 500 miles away in search of employment. They had tried for months without any success. Since leaving school they had been on training schemes and made application after application with no success. One broke down in tears as he related that he left his lovely wife and young baby not knowing if they had anything to eat. He was so embarrassed and demoralised because he could not provide for them.

We made room and shifted things around to accommodate them in our already crowded house and at our overcrowded table. They searched and searched in the days that followed. Promises of employment were given but nothing materialised. With some dismay I saw how the light in their eyes grew dimmer with each passing day, their hopes slowly disappearing, their dignity dented because they had to lodge with complete strangers and had not a pound between them. I came home one night to be told that they had left. My heart broke within me because we had not been able to alleviate their suffering. We never heard from them again but the memory of their earnest faces filled with such helplessness and pain, so young, haunts me still.

* * *

Bob was obviously a middle-class man. He was in his forties and was married with two teenage sons. Suddenly he was made redundant but, undaunted, he went in search of another job. Then he attended a retraining programme with high hopes that he would find an appropriate position before too long. The weeks passed into months and the months rolled into years. At the time I met the family, Bob was still looking and searching. Slowly but surely they began eating into their savings. They had to sell their house and some of their treasured belongings because they could no longer afford the mortgage and other expenses. The boys were at an important stage of their education but had to move with their parents as they rehoused themselves in another town where accommodation was cheaper.

Their studies were inevitably disrupted. One of the sons, who had been so well mannered and respectful, became increasingly hostile and aggressive. Bob and his wife visibly aged during this time. They lived in cramped rooms. Every day their hopes and aspirations grew weaker. Although he is willing to do any kind of work this man now lives in utter despair. His future seems to be a long and dreary gloom. He is a broken man struggling to hang on to his sanity.

* * *

These are by no means isolated examples. I come into contact with many such people every day in my inner city work in Great Britain, but it is also true in the rural areas. In the inner cities there are elderly people who freeze in the winter. We know widows who worked long after their retirement, faithfully serving the community and paying their taxes, but who now cannot afford to keep themselves and pay the poll tax. Being upright and honest people, and because they fear harassment from the authorities, they try to pay the poll tax and endure the humiliation of living on other people's charity. They looked forward with great anticipation to enjoying their twilight years but instead they are suffering the indignity of poverty and the pains of hunger.

Would you believe that in Britain in 1991 twenty percent of the population receive only 5.9 percent of the disposable income and this includes welfare benefits? Conversely the most affluent twenty percent of the population receive 42.2 percent of all disposable income. The underclass is growing.

The average debt of those going to advice bureaux in 1987 was £4,500 excluding mortgages. One Birmingham money advisory centre has estimated that they have 1000 young people applying for help each year. Most are unemployed, now with an average debt of £6,500. Consumer debt generally rose from £500 million in 1975 to over £30,000 million in 1986.

Where are all these people, victims of circumstance? They are right on our doorsteps, in our towns and cities of Great Britain. God is very concerned for the poor, underprivileged and disadvantaged people in Britain in 1991, as he was for the Israelites many thousands of years ago. God has not abandoned humanity. He has not given them up and he will still call into judgement those who disregard his principles and treat humanity as though they were cheap things, pieces of property.

WHY CARE?

There are over 400 references in the Bible to do with the poor. If we were to cut out all these, and the related verses, we would be left with a Bible full of holes. If we are concerned to be true to *all* the teaching of the Bible, we have to take note of those 400 references. What is this teaching? It is woven together around seven main strands:

1 God's intention at creation

In Genesis 1: 26–28 God revealed his original intention for humanity. He created humankind in his own image, investing them with value and dignity. They were to subdue and rule over all things instead of being oppressed. They were to reign in life, not live under the constant burden and pressure of poverty. In Acts 17: 26 we are told that 'from one man [God] made every nation of men': he created all people equal.

2 The shalom concept

In the Old Testament God communicated to his people by giving them many revelations of himself. These revelations reflected his holiness and justice, out of which his dealings with mankind was governed. The Old Testament concept of *shalom* is the same as the New Testament concept of salvation; it means wholeness. The people of Israel knew that God was offering them a quality of life that was holistic; it had to do with their health, welfare, peace and future.

3 The jubilee concept

In Leviticus 25: 10 it is decreed that in every fiftieth year all land was to be returned to the family who originally owned it. If members of that family had moved away, perhaps having sold themselves into slavery, they were free to return to their family property in that fiftieth year. Their original position and status was restored, their debts were cancelled. In this way the balance of ownership in society was maintained.

4 The call of the prophets

The whole thrust of the prophets was towards the freedom of the poor. Again and again they took up the cause of the poor against those who oppressed them. Isaiah was told to 'Raise your voice like a trumpet.

Declare to my people their rebellion.' And he proceeded to rebuke them for their religiosity and their hypocrisy. They would fast and humble themselves and come to God with their offerings, yet they would drive hard bargains with their workers, cheat them with their wages and keep them under the thumb. The Lord had enough of this hypocrisy, so he said to them,

> 'Is not this the kind of fasting I have chosen:
> to loose the chains of injustice
> and untie the cords of the yoke,
> to set the oppressed free
> and break every yoke?
> Is it not to share your food with the hungry
> and to provide the poor wanderer with shelter–
> when you see the naked, to clothe him,
> and not to turn away from your own flesh and blood?
> *Isaiah 58: 6–7*

Amos, the shepherd-prophet of the Old Testament, boldly proclaimed the cause of the poor against the religious bigots and oppressors of the poor of his day:

> 'I hate, I despise your religious feasts;
> I cannot stand your assemblies.
> . . . But let justice roll on like a river,
> righteousness like a never-failing stream!'
> *Amos 5: 21, 24*

It is so tragically possible for us to be religious and yet not real. Possible for us to have an outward show of godliness and yet lack its reality and the power, love and life of God within us. We can be immersed in religious activities, fasting, praying, singing, dancing and giving offerings, and yet God may be rebuking us as people unmoved in our hearts, untouched by the suffering and plight of the poor. We need to recapture God's heart for people, to feel what God feels for them, to experience, empathise and identify with their humiliation, pain and suffering.

5 The gospel command

The New Testament makes it very clear that, with the coming of Jesus, God was proclaiming a new era, the era of the kingdom. Jesus came to liberate people and bring them into a holistic experience with God. The provision of God for mankind was a whole gospel for the total person. This was what Jesus proclaimed when, at the beginning of his ministry, he said:

> 'The spirit of the Lord is on me
> because he has anointed me
> to preach good news to the poor.
> He has sent me to proclaim freedom for the prisoners
> and recovery of sight for the blind,
> to release the oppressed,
> to proclaim the year of the Lord's favour.'
>
> *Luke 4: 18–19*

The 'year of the Lord's favour' was a reference to the jubilee year – a year that brought good news to the poor, release to the captives and freedom to the downtrodden. The heart of God was so moved with compassion for those who were like sheep without a shepherd that he gave his only Son to bring about a much greater work of liberation. Jesus is good news to the poor!

When Jesus commissioned his disciples, he told them to go into every part of the world to make disciples and teach them all that he had taught them. Their words were no mere theories but were to be lived out in practice. In order to teach people about Jesus they had to practice what they preached – good news to the poor.

6 The example of the first Christians

Soon after the day of Pentecost, when 3000 people turned to Christ, the early apostles, acting on the instructions received from the Lord, formed those new Christians into a community. It was an obvious and natural outworking of the good news, a practical demonstration of it. It is recorded that they cared for one another and shared their earthly possessions with one another, to the end that none of them lacked anything (Acts 2 and 4).

7 The coming judgement

The Lord told his disciples that the son of man would return in glory, majesty and splendour. All the nations will be gathered before him and he will judge them on the basis of what they have done. He will separate the sheep from the goats. Those who have fed the hungry, cared for the stranger, clothed the naked and visited the sick and imprisoned will be divided from those who have not (Matthew 25: 31–46). His answer to perplexity from both sides will be, 'Whatever you did for one of the least of these brothers of mine, you did for me.'

Every time I read this passage I am challenged. I sometimes wonder if inadvertently I have turned Jesus away from my door. If unintentionally I passed him by without recognising him. The hungry person, the thirsty person, the imprisoned person, the sick and handicapped and helpless. I feel that we should learn to recognise Jesus in those people. To see Jesus in the eyes, to recognise that he is there with them, identifying with them. We need the same kind of compassion that will move us to reach out to those whom society has forgotten and passed by. In the light of eternity can we do less? After all, when all the riches and the splendour, glitter and glamour of this world have vanished, what will we have left in eternity? Only those things which we have done to alleviate the suffering and to ameliorate the needs of those who are heavy laden and disadvantaged.

Paul writing to the Corinthians emphasised to them the value of the body of Christ and that each member in the body is both significant and valuable (1 Corinthians 12: 12–26). No one should be despised, counted weak or treated with less honour than another. It is in the context of community that we find our greatest fulfilment and opportunity to serve.

THE CALL TO ACTION

Whose responsibility are the poor? If the church will not rise up and take action then I ask you who will? We can pretend that they are not there, continue with our usual agenda and ignore the destitute masses around us. We can shut them out of our lives and create a little world of our own. The church is known for its ability to be insular and to lock itself out from the real needs of real people. We need to rise up as a prophetic people and take prophetic action.

In the face of such overwhelming odds and tremendous need what can you or I really do?

- *Start just where you are.*
- *Start with what you have.* When the Lord called Moses to go and deliver Israel out of the hand of the mighty Pharaoh he asked, 'What is that in your hand? (Exodus 4: 2.) Start with what is in your hand. God requires no more and no less.
- *Mobilize all your resources*, human as well as financial.
- *Organise yourself*, even if it means changing your agenda, meetings and programmes. Make sensible and appropriate plans: do some research to identify the particular needs in your community and make specific plans to meet those needs. It may be that in your area there are some elderly people that need someone to do their shopping or repair a window or someone to relieve their loneliness – simply someone to speak to. Maybe some young people need an extra hand to help them with their school lessons or somebody who will make them feel important and not rejects of society.

There are so many ways in which we can do little things for little people, practical things for ordinary people, things that require our dying to ourselves, making sacrifices, giving our time and energies to serve others. But at the end of the day we will be empowering the powerless, enabling the weak, serving the needy; we will be doing it to Jesus.

- *Get to the root causes.* Someone has said, 'when people go hungry it is not because there is a shortage of food it is because there is a shortage of justice.' And a bishop in Latin America said, 'When I give them food they say I am a saint, when I ask why there is no food they label me a communist.' Sooner or later, we need to get down to the root causes of poverty and not deal only with the symptoms.

If we were to get to the heart of the matter we would find things that are very disturbing indeed, things that would make you cringe and may even cause you to feel embarrassed to be a human being. Digging a little beneath the surface we may discover that there are political institutions and systems created to keep the mass of people living only at a certain level. Systems are so designed that it is almost impossible for some people in the community to rise above certain prescribed financial ceilings. Some laws are cleverly designed in order to protect vested interests. Rules and regulations are enforced which make it almost impossible for some people in society to make any headway. Commercial enterprises and multi-national companies employ people to devise ways and means of exploiting the poorest in society.

To make any long-term headway, the church of God must go beyond the superficial. It must seek out the real causes of poverty and unemployment and adequately deal with them if we are to bring this kind of tyranny to an end.

11

REACHING OUT

In the surrounding streets where Muriel and I live there are people from different races, colours and backgrounds. Being virtual strangers in the area when we first arrived, we felt a bit shy and also afraid that if we made friendly overtures we may be rebuffed and rejected. There are teenagers, old age pensioners, blacks, whites, Asians. We have been involved in missionary work for thirty years and helped all sorts of people, invited people from all nationalities into our home, and preached across the country encouraging others to reach out, especially to people who are different from themselves. So, as the weeks went by we began to feel very uncomfortable with our own shyness! We decided to do what we have done elsewhere and what we ask others to do. And the Lord surprised us. As we knocked on doors and greeted people on the streets, enquiring after their welfare, we found they were willing to talk. Now our neighbours are our friends. I am glad we had the courage to do on our doorstep what we advocate in our cities and countries!

God cares for the foreigner. He loves them as he loved the children of Israel in Egypt. He is moved with the same compassion that moved him to deliver the children of Israel out of Pharaoh's bondage and set them free. Every person is a spiritual and social being and as such has both spiritual and social needs. Each one needs to belong, to be affirmed, to be appreciated and also to feel that others need him or her. God therefore asked his messianic community to respect the fact that all people are created in his image:

> 'Do not ill-treat an alien or oppress him, for you were aliens in Egypt.' *Exodus 22:21*

> 'When an alien lives with you in your land, do not ill-treat him. The alien living with you must be treated as one of your native-born. Love him as yourself, for you were aliens in Egypt. I am the Lord your God.
>
> Do not use dishonest standards when measuring length, weight or quantity. Use honest scales and honest weights, an honest ephah and an honest hin. I am the Lord your God, who brought you out of Egypt.' *Leviticus 19:33–36*

Who are the 'aliens' in our communities today? There are at least four types of person we can identify:

- Someone who is not a relative.
- Someone from another race, colour, culture or country.

- Someone who is alienated from society, family or friends.
- Someone who is shut off, frozen out of other people's company. He or she is not part of an 'in group'.

God commanded the Israelites to treat such people with great love and care; not to show them hostility or handle them with aggression, nor deal with them insincerely.

Many people are very polite but not sincere. People of all classes, races and cultures need genuine acceptance not superficial accommodation. Have you ever been in a company of people where all is polite and happy, then someone leaves and to your surprise someone sighs or makes a rude comment, as if to say, 'good riddance!'? I have, and I have also felt disgusted at the hypocrisy of it all.

A friend and I used to meet regularly to pray. We had very lovely times of fellowship and felt we had a great relationship going. He invited me to drop in any time at his home. I took him at his word. After a few visits another friend, ever so polite, informed me that my first friend was embarrassed by my going to his house, but he was too much of a gentleman to tell me. For crying out loud! I hadn't been visiting him *daily*, maybe once a week, and never for a meal. And it was his idea! But why, I wondered, didn't he *say* what he really *meant*? People are very sensitive and they easily pick up when they are being patronised. Likewise, they also discern when someone is genuinely interested in them for their own sake.

'POSITIVE DISCRIMINATION'

There are several ideas present in these verses that give a positive indication of how God feels about foreigners, strangers and aliens. There is both a negative and positive aspect. Things not to do and things to do. The command, 'Do not ill-treat an alien or oppress him' implies that the opposite action is the appropriate action to take. In other words, we could restate the command as, 'Treat an alien well and do all that you can to promote his well being.' Or, put yet another way, 'Love your neighbour as yourself.' We must do what is just and right towards them, relieving their burdens instead of ill-treating them, oppressing them and doing wrong to them. The Lord looks for a high standard of 'positive discrimination' from us. He mentions three particular things we should be doing:

- *Treat the foreigner as a fellow citizen.* Give him the same respect and equality as you would a member of the indigenous population. Make no distinction because of his race, colour, culture, creed, social or financial status. Make him feel at home! Help the foreigner to have a sense of belonging and provide him with a context within which he can find an identity. Do not treat him as an outcast but as a friend and brother.

- *Love the foreigner as yourself.* This kind of love is not dependent on the merits or demerits of the recipient. It is love for love's sake. The things you like for yourself you must also desire for others, even the foreigner. Love from a heart that bears no grudge, harbours no resentment, cherishes no preconceptions, nurtures no prejudice that may hinder you from being friendly and kindly disposed to him. There is no room here for any hatred or even a silent wish that the aliens had 'never come to our land'. The whole weight of the Bible's teaching emphasises that true love for God and one's neighbour (alien) is the essence of all our worship and service.

• *Make every effort to help the foreigner thrive.* We know how vulnerable and stupid we feel when in a foreign country on holiday or on business, and can't quite get to grips with the currency. Most British people are convinced the locals are out to take as much advantage of this confusion as possible! And in this country, where everything is familiar and easy to us, it is easy to stand by and watch a foreigner flounder. Again and again God counselled the Israelites that their responsibility was to uphold truth and justice at all times. All their dealings with others must be stamped with integrity. Far from allowing cheating, corruption or underhand dealing to be done, they were to show great sensitivity and consideration to those especially vulnerable to such things. God's love reaches out to all, irrespective of who they are or from where they have come; so must ours be.

OPPRESSION AND ILL-TREATMENT

In Egypt there had been one law for the Egyptians and another for the Hebrews. There was not a proper appreciation of the contribution they had made to the development of Egypt, which became a very great and powerful nation. How easily and how soon people forget. Not only were they taken for granted but they were despised and rejected, their rights taken away. It was this scenario that the Lord was asking his people to remember so that they would not commit the same crimes or their equivalent against people in their midst who may now be vulnerable, weak and helpless; people who served them and who were obligated to them, people who depended on their good will for their prosperity and development.

There are many ways by which people, even in our society, can be oppressed and ill-treated. Britain is a world in miniature. The once glorious empire has been thrown into reverse gear and thousands of its subjects have come home to the Motherland, to their capital. Ten percent of Britain's population are from ethnic minorities drawn from the different colonies of the empire: six million people from different cultures, races and religions. Truly a multi-racial, multi-cultural and multi-religious society. Unfortunately, the indigenous peoples of Britain have not yet been able to readjust to post-empire life.

When the empire was at the height of its power peoples from Europe travelled out to the various countries and stamped their will upon nation after nation, controlling their economies, exporting their goods. They had a ready and free market. They imported raw materials at the price determined by them. Now that all those privileges and sources no longer exist they think that their quality of life is threatened by the presence of all these once-conquered peoples of the world who were once very much their slaves and servants.

Instead of living in fear and suspicion, generating

hostility and aggression, we need to hear what God said to the children of Israel and learn some crucial lessons that may help us live in peace, harmony and partnership with one other.

There are many ways by which we oppress people who live among us and who come from a different country, class, race, colour or background. Here are some of the common ways this happens:

- *We deprive them of certain rights and privileges.* It is a well-established fact that many people of ethnic origin cannot advance in society further than certain levels, however qualified they might be for positions of leadership and management. Their promotion is blocked because it is an unwritten policy that certain people should not be promoted into the higher levels of management. This may seem far fetched, and sometimes we are accused of making mountains out of molehills. There is, however, well-documentated evidence to show that this is not just a theory but an everyday happening in society.

- *We subject them to physical and verbal abuse.* Children are subjected to ugly remarks. They are called 'niggers' and 'non achievers'. Groups of people like the National Front go around in gangs to harass and beat the innocent, weak and defenseless. 'Paki bashing', 'Asian hunting' and other things are well known.

Sometimes harassment comes from the most unexpected quarters. A young couple who came to seek higher education at London university were subjected to some of the most unbelievable harassment. The wife was pregnant and they already had a two-year-old baby.

They were tenants in a block of flats and their neighbours took exception to them. Water was poured into their flat, super-glue stuck into their keyhole, verbal abuses hurled at them and once dogs were set on them. Eventually it became so unbearable that we had to rescue them and move them out into other accommodation.

• *We deny them normal legal rights.* Many times false allegations are made against people who are innocent. They are dragged into police stations and some of them are convicted. Now sitting in prison, although not guilty, they still cannot prove their innocence. There are many cases where people are framed and set up. One can hardly believe that these things happen in such an enlightened, modern society as ours. How devious and cruel we can be to each other!

There was a young boy who was sexually assaulted and molested, but was too frightened to say anything. No one knew until he became sick and infected. When the matter was brought to the right authorities the accusations were not even received. He was a young *black* boy.

• *We deny them a fair chance to succeed.* A young lady I know very well was sent by an agency in answer to a request made by a firm of lawyers. She was well qualified for the job. She turned up as arranged and as soon as the manager came out and saw that she was black he made a hasty retreat, without even so much as a greeting. Later he sent out one of his subordinates to inform her that she was not needed. Needless to say there was no explanation or apology.

We oppress people when we make them feel that they

are second-class citizens and not worth our time of day. We oppress people when we do not pay them wages that they deserve. Employers take advantage of the foreigner's need for ready money and because they cannot do better for themselves they end up working long hours underpaid.

We cannot afford to turn a blind eye to this situation. We do well to make every effort to reconcile our differences and seek to understand one another. Helping one another we can work together for a better community and to give our children a future.

RACISM

Racism is an attitude of the heart and a state of the mind. It is that which makes one feel superior to the other, it has no boundary and no one is immune to it, nor does anyone have a monopoly on it. We are all creatures of prejudice to a greater or lesser degree. Racism is a complex state of mind, often born out of mistaken pride. Sometimes it is deep insecurity which drives people to assert themselves, especially over others who are less fortunate than they are. They do this without paying much attention to the rights or wrongs of the matter. Justice and fairness does not enter into the scheme of things. The overriding passion that motivates them is the need for self preservation and to service their vested interest.

Racism is a definite bias against other people's manners, customs, culture, class and status. The ugliest manifestation of it is when people dislike and even hate you *just because you are different*. We are all entitled to our preferences, we do not have to agree on everything. We do not even have to like everyone and every thing. Everyone should be free to enjoy his or her particular 'cup of tea'. The sin and problem, however, is when our preferences become our prejudices, our likes becomes antagonisms and our disagreement becomes animosity. The roots of prejudice can be so deeply buried in our inner self that we don't always recognise its presence. In unguarded moments when we least suspect it, it pops up its ugly head to remind us that we are but humans. Most times we are surprised and sometimes even embarrassed when this happens.

There are different forms of racism and oppression of other peoples. In every case it cannot be regarded as anything but sin. It is sin because:

- It is an insult to God's work of creation so wonderfully, carefully and beautifully made.
- It robs people of their dignity and value.
- It diminishes their humanity.
- It promotes hurt and pain, hatred, bloodshed and a whole list of other atrocities that are not worthy of the species called human beings.
- Within the body of Christ it hinders the function of the new humanity for which Jesus Christ died.
- It is an evidence of our fallen nature and a sure sign of our rebellion against God.

There are covert and overt forms of racism. Some people appear so polite, so warm and welcoming but in reality they do not really want you around. They do and say all the right things but inwardly they do not mean it, secretly they despise and dislike you. There is also a form of inverted racism. People who are victims of injustice, who have been on the receiving end of racist policies and attitudes or have suffered violence and have been denied their rights, can develop strong reactions. Inverted racism develops from the feeling that enough is enough. Like a wounded animal reacting against its tormentors, the hurt and pain run so deep that it breeds feelings of hostility and aggression.

'I can't take it any more, Philip, I feel as though I would collapse.' She broke down into tears. She was born here, a young mother with three children, struggling to keep her head above water and to hold her family together. She is harassed, beaten up, subjected to obscenities, they bang her door, pelt her windows. A defenseless woman who had been taken to court when others should have been. She is now experiencing some calm because we were able to get her some proper legal representation after the solicitor she was first given did not turn up in court. Instead he sent a letter to the magistrate advising against her.

There are other stories like this which fill one with horror and pain. Sometimes the only way people can retain their sanity is to retaliate.

On the receiving end

When a person is humiliated and made to surrender her dignity, and when her sense of justice is violated she could respond in one of three ways:

- Resign herself and accept the situation as it is.
- Curl up and die.

• Protest and fight for her corner, to 'give as good as you get'.

The question must be asked: What should the Christian do? Naturally the people of God cannot retaliate in kind and behave as those who do not know the grace of God. We can learn some lessons from the Israelites.

• *Take it to God.* The Israelites cried out to God when their protests, delegations and arguments failed. And God heard them, came down and fought for them and brought them deliverance from their captors.

This may seem a weak answer. It may be even be regarded by some as the coward's way out, a 'cop-out' if you like, a means by which you avoid the real issues instead of confronting them head on. But more is wrought by prayer than people imagine. It is a powerful piece of action which does not take away our personhood but equips us to face problems with fortitude. There is no greater example given us than that of the Lord Jesus himself. What seemed to be defeat for Jesus and an overwhelming victory for Satan, when Jesus hung on the cross, we now know in hindsight to have been the greatest hour of victory for all mankind. Despite appearances at the time, no greater victory will ever be won and no defeat will be so devastating as that which Jesus dealt to the forces of darkness and the devil, when he seemed at his weakest. God was working in a way hidden to the world.

• *Forgive.* It was Jesus who said that we must rejoice when we are persecuted, forgive those who wrong us and learn to love those who oppress us as Christ loves us. To forgive and rejoice in persecution is powerful and never fails to have effect, as Martin Luther King and Gandhi demonstrated. Ask the East German and Chinese Christians. Missionaries have been martyred in South America and today whole families, villages and tribes have turned to Jesus as a result of their witness.

Is forgiveness the coward's way out? No, my friend, it is God's way of liberating us from the inside to get rid from our own hearts, minds and spirits the tensions, pressure, hurt and pain that others have inflicted on us. We need to be free in order to be whole. Before God can use us to solve problems outside ourselves he needs to help us to solve the problems inside ourselves. Before we can break the chains that bind others we need to break the chains within that bind us. Before we can be salt in the wound of the enemy we need to find healing in our own wounds and before we can bring light into the darkness and corruption of this world we need the light of God to fill our own hearts and minds. To release our bitterness and to forgive our oppressors is not the coward's way out. It is God's way to sort us out and give us victory over ourselves. It puts us in control rather than letting us continue to be the helpless victims of circumstance, tossed about by violent winds. To forgive and to love is to rise above the meanness of others. It is to be a better person. Not that bad as a line of attack, is it? Instead of suffering silently and internalising our anger it is healthier to pray it out and pour it out at the throne of God. He understands.

Does this mean that we accept their oppression and meekly surrender without a whimper? Forever having to endure these heavy burdens? No, not at all. Like Moses and the children of Israel there is room for us to protest.

• *Spiritual warfare.* We are to take prophetic action, without betraying our faith or compromising our values. We know that the kingdom of God is not of this world. The weapons of our warfare are therefore not of this world either but they are mighty to pull down the strongholds of evil. It simply means that we wage our war from a different level with different weapons. We wage war from higher ground, just as Moses, Aaron and Hur did when the children of Israel were attacked by the Amalekites.

This is not meek surrender but battle of another dimension.

• *Non-violent confrontation.* There is place for prayer but also place for spirit-inspired and spirit-directed action. Moses went directly to the throne and demanded of Pharaoh, 'Let my people go.' At first Pharaoh and his officers did not even give him the time of day. Did he give up? No. He went again and again. When protests, pleas and appeals failed he brought God in to work some pretty serious miracles which made Pharaoh surrender. The best form of peaceful co-existence with hostile neighbours is co-belligerence by fervent prayer, non-violent protest and some supernatural demonstration of God's power.

LEGALISED AND INSTITUTIONAL RACISM

Some people use their influence in politics to protect their interests and preserve the *status quo*. They create institutions and design laws that will serve their own causes and promote the interest of the dominant members of society instead of serving the weak, helpless, struggling, voiceless ones.

Others manipulate the economy and financial institutions to ensure that the poor always will remain poor enough to serve those who are better off. They can come so far but no further. They invent programmes to pacify the sufferers but provide no long-term solutions. The root causes are never confronted or resolved. Laws are initiated which restrict people's freedom of movement. They are not free to choose where to live, what career to pursue, where to go, whom to marry.

Planet earth is filled with divisions along racial, tribal, economic and class lines. It is not just history – 'past story' – it is 'now story'. There are still Indian reservations in North and South America. People are not free to occupy even their own land. It is illegal for them to venture beyond the boundaries that were set by those who have conquered them. Even today whole villages are bulldozed, people burnt out of their homelands and wholesale massacre committed, all in the interests of wealthy companies and persons.

South Africa's reprehensible apartheid system has, until very recently, been fully legalised and even sanctified by some so-called Christian theologians. They are 'logians' all right but I cannot find 'theos' in their doctrines. The caste system of India, intertribal rivalries in

Africa, the dilemma of Northern Ireland, the eternal struggle between the Jews and the Arabs, the north-south disparity, the black and white divide, Islam versus Christianity versus communism versus . . . This is the inheritance which we leave for the next generation to take into the twenty-first century.

Is there any real answer? It would seem that the whole world is held to ransom by men of prejudice; bigots and charlatans who consider themselves to be superior and have a God-given right to rule over all they can conquer. Their greed and prejudice seem to know no bounds. It is really a conquest of the bullies, isn't it?

It only proves that the spirit of Pharaoh lives on. But it also fills me with hope that just as Pharaoh's day of reckoning came there is also a day of reckoning for all those who have dealt unjustly with their fellow men, ill-treated and oppressed them. The God who was greatly moved by the plight of the Israelites made sure that he impressed upon their hearts that they should never cultivate such prejudices and perpetrate such crimes against other fellow human beings. To take advantage of the stranger in your midst in order to feed your ego or line your pockets must be wrong. Pharaoh used the Israelites to make himself cities, but he did not reckon with God.

THE CHRISTIAN'S RESPONSE

What should the Christian response be? If we remain silent we become conspirators with those who perpetrate these crimes against humanity. To adopt racist attitudes is to sink to the level of the perpetrators and become partners in their crime. To fight fire with fire solves nothing, only creates greater conflagration. To retreat and withdraw is to display an uncaring attitude and lack of concern which does not reflect the heart of the God who delivered Israel from Egypt. There must be a higher way, a better way, a God's way.

In the final analysis such large-scale wrongs will only be righted when the supernatural power of God is released in our society. Like Israel, we long to see divine intervention that will bring deliverance to all men and women, such an unprecedented move of God that will not only change the situation of men and women everywhere but will also change the hearts and attitudes of people. I long to see a revolution of love, an outpouring of the Spirit of God in such unprecedented measure that the tide of evil will be turned back. Where are the Wesleys, Luthers, Wilberforces, Shaftsburys and Booths of today? Where are the people who will offer themselves unreservedly to God to be real ambassadors for liberation and will fight for justice for all?

God will bring about the final completion of his plan for humankind. But in the meantime we have a choice. We can either be part of the solution or part of the problem. We can be partners in the plan of God or we can become a forgotten piece of history. I would rather be a part of the solution.

To be effective agents for change we need to get to grips with two broad options. Firstly we need to ask, what are the things that contribute to and perpetrate racism – and am I part of the problem? We sometimes do not realise how our attitudes or actions are helping to aggravate a situation rather than relieve it. Then, secondly, we need to look at some practical ways for becoming partners with God in working for justice, equality and wholeness for all people.

Partners or problems?

These are some factors which contribute to racial tensions between different peoples, and even lead to abuse.

- *Ignorance.* We neither take the time nor make the effort to know each other properly. We do not know each other's history, customs, family backgrounds and in many cases we do not really care. We adopt the attitude, 'It's none of our business anyway.' 'What are they doing here?' 'They might as well go back home' – wherever home is. In some cases we do not even know each other's names, though we live next door or just across the street from each other. We are content to form our opinions from things we suspect or hear through rumours, read in the papers, hear on the radio, and see on the television. From these we proceed to form images of people. We place them in pigeon holes and we stereotype them. It is easier to deal with people if we can put them in certain categories. It is only as we really get to know people on a personal basis that we may surprise ourselves to find they, too, are ordinary human beings with dreams and aspirations that are not too unlike our own. Ignorance, they say, is bliss. It might be blissful, but is it *right*?

- *Arrogance.* Arrogant people adopt a superior attitude and stance. They are always right, they know everything and they always know best. It often manifests itself in haughtiness. They look down on others, no one is as clever or good as they are. They despise anything that does not originate from 'their' authors, composers, inventors, scientists, engineers, doctors, etc. 'We' are the best. Even when statistics show otherwise. No one can do it as well as we can. Such people are either bullies, insecure or conceited. Arrogance does not help in creating better relationships between people of different nationalities.

• *Insensitivity*. Isn't it amazing how insensitive some of us can be to others? We can be so unfeeling and crude, we do not regard the feelings, needs, situations or circumstances in which others may find themselves. We cannot relate to people outside our own context. We live only to please ourselves, without any thought for others. And, as long as we get what we want, it does not matter who gets hurt in the process. We end up saying and doing things that hurt and offend, and can only cause greater gaps to develop.

Sometimes our insensitivity leads us to insult people's intelligence. Can you imagine some of the questions that are asked during our travels? First, people will ask, 'Where are you from?' You promptly answer. Then they ask you, 'What is it like?' And in rapid succession the questions come. 'Do you have snow? Do you have cats? Do you have dogs?' And the list goes on and on. But, wait for it! The real shock comes when they condescend to ask you, 'Do your cows give milk?' 'Do they eat grass?' 'Do your cats have kittens?' If it was not so insulting to one's intelligence it would be laughable. Actually we do have some really hilarious times. But there is no need to make jokes at each other's expense or to make remarks about people's food, dress, culture, or customs. Most such remarks are negative and are always measured only by our own customs.

Practical suggestions

Sometimes, out of the goodness of our hearts and with all good intentions, we seek to lend a helping hand, to give charity to others with a view to alleviating their burdens. However, if the impact of the good we do is to be maintained we must at all cost avoid patronisation and paternalism. Our good must build up not break down. It must be kept inconspicuous.

We must learn to treat people as equals not as objects for our pity and sympathy. It is important that we learn to accept people in their own right as people and not look on them as second-class citizens or poor cousins.

It is also necessary for us to avoid tokenism. We should not use people for the sake of justifying ourselves or appearing to be doing the right thing in the eyes of others. We should not use people to provide us with a way of escape from blame or to present a picture that is not real. Though *you* may be fooled into thinking your motives are right, those whom you are 'helping' will see through any superficiality, and when they do they will despise you for it. Though they may receive what you give without saying anything because of their unfortunate position or because of some obligation, they will be very deeply hurt and will feel reduced. When we take their sense of worth and value from people we not only demoralise them but we undermine their confidence and leave them mortally wounded, sometimes for life.

So, if we are to work for peace and harmony and partnership there are some practical things which we must seek to do:

- *Identify problem areas.* We need to identify the areas of problem and need in our own church or community. A helpful exercise would be to find out what different races, cultures and classes are living within your own community. It might surprise you! You will probably find there are more than you imagined. In a conference when we did this exercise among thirty people we found that in some small communities there were over twenty-five different nationalities living together.

- *Educate ourselves.* We need to understand the underlying causes of these problems, and the issues at their heart, if our subsequent action is to be strategic.

- *Repent.* We need to repent of some things. Let us recognise the areas where we have failed people, maybe go back into our history and see where we have wronged, exploited or even hurt people. Identify with your own history, but instead of feeling guilty bring it to God and seek forgiveness. If at all possible, make restitution. But whatever you do, do not go around with a guilt complex. Get rid of it.

- *Reach out.* We need to reach out to other people who are different from us. Make friends with them, visit their homes, invite them into your home, share a meal together.

- *Accept people as they are.* We need to accept people as they are in their own uniqueness and not as we would like them to be. We cannot ask people to be converted and to become like us before we are prepared to receive them. This is the mistake that the Jews made when they demanded that Gentile Christians ought first to become Jews and take on board all their cultural package if they wanted to belong to the church. They saw themselves as the sole custodians of the grace of God. It was wrong then; it is wrong now. The predominant group should not seek to subsume the minority group. Whites have no right to ask the blacks to become whites before they are accepted in their company, nor do the blacks have any right to ask the whites to become black before they are accepted. Whether Asian, Chinese – whatever our nationality we have no right to demand that the one become what the other is. But we can respect each other, value each other for what we are, learn from each other and be enriched by each other.

• *Live among oppressed people.* We can demonstrate God's love for oppressed and marginalised communities by going to live among them, planting chunles, creating a kingdom community, initiating youth clubs, care and support groups, and possibly even creating job programmes.

• *Do not impose our own agendas.* It is important that we do not seek to impose our wills, our ways, customs, likes and dislikes onto each other but that we allow each person the freedom to be himself or herself. We do not need to compromise on essential issues, and the heart of the gospel need not be tampered with, but we need to learn how to 'become all things to all men that we might win some' (see 1 Corinthians 9: 18–23). If we are to bring reconciliation, become agents for change and vehicles to bring in the Kingdom of God, then we must learn how to treat each other with respect.

We *can* work towards being real friends. We *can* develop a sense of partnership based on mutual respect for each other. The cross-fertilisation of ideas can only be mutually enriching.

- *Hold discussion groups.* We can host discussion groups, inviting a wide variety of concerned neighbours and acquaintances, with a view to finding solutions and practical answers to particular problems. Action groups can be set up out of such discussions, to make things happen.

- *Protest.* There is biblical precedent for loyal, but thought-out protests. Elijah confronted King Ahab about his unjust taking of property (1 Kings 21); Amos (see chapters 1–6) and Jeremiah (see chapters 5) protested about corruption at all levels of society. There are many other examples too.

- *Make representations.* We can come together to make representations to those in authority, for the poor and powerless. We should befriend those who find themselves in the 'underclass', as Jesus did.

- *Pray.* Prayer is where it all starts. Not only should we pray on our own, but we can form prayer groups to intercede and engage in spiritual warfare.

How often we hear people saying, 'We do not have that problem in our area.' Many of Britain's indigenous population do not yet fully appreciate that Britain is a multi-cultural, multi-racial and multi-religious nation, nor have they really considered the full implications and issues that arise from this. We so often move only in our own spheres among people who are just like us, so that our knowledge is restricted to the little world we build around ourselves. We need to dispell our inadequate ideas of each other and learn to come out of our little self-made worlds to discover and explore the world around us. We could each one make a valuable contribution for the future and the benefit of the next generation. Let us treat one another with love as brothers and sisters, and as friends. This is the crux of God's command to Israel and to us.

If we were to be catapulted forward to the time when all things would have reached their climax, what would we see? John had the privilege of seeing the end of things. When the curtains of time were drawn back and he was permitted a glimpse into that eternal world, this is what he saw:

> 'I looked and there before me was a great multitude that no one could count, from every nation, tribe, people and language, standing before the throne and in front of the Lamb. They were wearing white robes and were holding palm branches in their hands. And they cried out with a loud voice:
> "Salvation belongs to our God, who sits on the throne, and to the Lamb." ' *Revelation 7: 9–10*

Let us live for the Lamb and for that day when we shall all stand before his throne, one people without prejudice and distinction; God's people.

12

THE GOLDEN CALF SYNDROME

God knew that the Israelites did not stand a chance in a million of reaching their destiny, inheriting the promise and reaching their full potential unless they made God the single focus of their hearts. No distraction, no diversions; total allegiance. The God who redeemed them is the only one who could make such a claim, but they owed all that they were and had to him. This is the reason why God told them again and again, 'Do not make any gods to be alongside me; do not make for yourselves gods of silver or gods of gold' (Exodus 20:23).

God was not merely providing them with a list of prohibitions nor was he just trying to reinforce in their minds the idea of monotheism. He was issuing them with both a call and a warning. A call for them to pledge their absolute allegiance to him, and a warning of the way the society would crumble and fall if they forgot this and took on instead the values and practices of the nations around them. God was to have first place in their thinking. They were to be totally obedient to him in word, thought and deed.

This was not for selfish reasons, as though God is dependent on our fellowship, worship and obedience. God needs nothing from us for his own completeness and fulfilment but he knows that when our hearts are divided we stray away from him and become easy prey for the devil. If we share our lives with other things, and we drift outside the boundaries that he has placed around us for our protection, we cannot expect him to defend us, protect and provide for us. If we move away from him we cannot be shielded from the attacks of the enemy. The quickest way to forfeit our rights and lose his presence is to switch to some other god.

So with these warnings ringing in their ears, what did they do? Not many days after, they were bowing down to a golden calf made with their own hands:

> 'When the Lord finished speaking to Moses on Mount Sinai, he gave him the two tablets of the Testimony, the tablets of stone inscribed by the finger of God.
>
> When the people saw that Moses was so long in coming down from the mountain, they gathered around Aaron and said, "Come, make us gods who will go before us. As for this fellow Moses who brought us up out of Egypt, we don't know what has happened to him."
>
> Aaron answered them, "Take off the gold ear-rings that your wives, your sons and your daughters are wearing, and bring them to me." So all the people took off their ear-rings and brought them to Aaron. He took what they handed him and made it into an

> idol cast in the shape of a calf, fashioning it with a tool. Then they said, "These are your gods, O Israel, who brought you up out of Egypt."
>
> When Aaron saw this, he built an altar in front of the calf and announced, "Tomorrow there will be a festival to the Lord." So the next day the people rose early and sacrificed burnt offerings and presented fellowship offerings. Afterwards they sat down to eat and drink and got up to indulge in revelry.' *Exodus 31:18–32:6*

Today, millions worship at the altar of the god, materialism, the god of gold and silver. Just like the Israelites, they are caught up in a frenzied dance, and are drunk with the sweet wine of making money and acquiring possessions. It is mindlessly indulgent to satisfy the inner craving for material things and give little or no thought to the true purpose of life.

But how could the *children of Israel* have fallen from such heights to such depths, from such glory to utter disgrace? A people that promised so much ended up in such unmitigated disaster. When Moses confronted Pharaoh he said, 'Let my people go, so that they may hold a festival to me in the wilderness' (Exodus 5:1). I wonder what Pharaoh would have thought if he saw them now. They were celebrating a festival all right but it was not to God. It was to a golden calf, resembling one of the many gods that they had in Egypt. They could have done that in Egypt anyway! They didn't need to make such a dramatic exit and go through all the trouble to move out in the wilderness. They were free to join the Egyptians in their idol worship.

Sometimes we lose sight of our real calling as the

people of God, and we drift into things which we know to be wrong, and even despise. The children of Israel went from the worship of Yahweh their deliverer, provider, healer and warrior in battle, to the worship of a beautiful dumb idol. No wonder Moses was so distraught when he beheld the spectacle. Moses reacted with total disbelief and shock:

> 'Moses turned and went down the mountain with the two tablets of the Testimony in his hands. They were inscribed on both sides, front and back. The tablets were the work of God; the writing was the writing of God, engraved on the tablets.
>
> When Joshua heard the noise of the people shouting, he said to Moses, "There is the sound of war in the camp."
>
> Moses replied:
> "It is not the sound of victory,
> it is not the sound of defeat;
> it is the sound of singing that I hear."
>
> When Moses approached the camp and saw the calf and the dancing, his anger burned and he threw the tablets out of his hands, breaking them to pieces at the foot of the mountain. And he took the calf they had made and burned it in the fire; then he ground it to powder, scattered it on the water and made the Israelites drink it.
>
> He said to Aaron, "What did these people do to you, that you led them into such great sin?"
>
> "Do not be angry, my lord," Aaron answered. "You know how prone these people are to evil. They said to me, 'Make us gods who will go before us. As for this fellow Moses who brought us up out of Egypt, we don't know what has happened to him.' So I told them, 'Whoever has any gold jewellery,

> take it off.' Then they gave me the gold, and I threw it into the fire, and out came this calf!" '
>
> *Exodus 32:15–24*

This was one of those rare moments in Moses' life when he really got angry. So angry that he smashed the two tablets he brought down from the mountain. Such is the effect of idol worship in the courts of heaven and to all godly men and women everywhere. To make gold and silver the god we worship is the very height of folly, especially for a people with such great heritage, a people who should know better.

FROM GOD TO GOLD

They exchanged Yahweh for a chunk of dazzling gold. Solid but cold, uncaring and unfeeling. The idea was not really a new one; it was borrowed from the Egyptians. The young bull calf was an Egyptian symbol of fertility, prosperity and strength. They were happy to pin all their future hopes for prosperity, growth and strength as a nation on this golden piece of art, just as we today depend on gold for the well being and prosperity of our nation. Materialism indeed can and does provide a sense of security. We can see, feel and handle it. We know what is involved; we can quantify it. Trusting in gold does not seem as risky as believing in something or someone you cannot see.

Perhaps we need to be reminded that in the eternal perspective, 'our light and momentary troubles are achieving for us an eternal glory that far outweigh them all. So we fix our eyes not on what is seen, but on what is unseen. For what is seen is temporary, but what is unseen is eternal' (2 Corinthians 4:17–18). That which is *now* invisible to us is in fact far more real and significant than that which is visible, for the visible things of this world will all evaporate like a mist. But the eternal things which we have in God are for ever, they never pass away.

Yes, I agree that money can buy many of the creature comforts that we need. But what do we do when we are lonely and in despair, when we are weary and wounded, when we are distressed and burdened, when our heart cries out for a friendly shoulder on which to lean? What then? We are left only with the cold, solid, uncaring, unfeeling things. The cold fact is that houses, lands, cars, bank balances, works of art, or whatever material possessions we may have, cannot feel what we feel, cannot touch the inner parts of our true self. This is when we need to fall back on our God who offers us his friendship and his fatherhood and we should never seek to replace him with any thing else or anyone else.

Look at the folly of the children of Israel. They gambled their long term future for short term gains. They were too impatient, they could not wait for Moses to reappear. They sacrificed the ultimate for the immediate. They grasped the tangible thing which they could see rather than believe and trust in God whom they could experience but could not see. 'Seeing is believing!' I can hear them say. Lots of people still say that today. They forgot the real issues and problems which were confronting them, and instead of getting down to the heart of the matter, they opted for temporary alternative relief.

The irony of the whole scenario is that they covered

it all with a good dose of religiosity. They built an altar, offered sacrifices, sang, danced, worshipped. Aaron actually proclaimed, 'Tomorrow there will be a festival to the Lord.' He sought to retain some modicum of his own self respect and put a religious face on the whole exercise, as if to say we have not *really* forgotten Jehovah; tomorrow we shall worship this golden calf in honour of Jehovah. What unreality! What a farce!

I guess it made them feel a little better, although they had committed so great a sin against the Lord. They probably thought, as many do today, that once they had done what they considered to be their 'religious duty', they could not be too bad after all. 'God surely understands,' they probably claimed, as again many do today. God is a matter of convenience, not a matter of conviction and commitment.

GOLD ASHES

The tragic thing about this episode in the Israelites' history is the fact that their gold turned into ashes and evaporated without trace. When their lives were in ruins, buried in the ashes of the brick kilns of Egypt, God raised them up and out of their ashes brought golden qualities into their lives, experience and worship. They chose to exchange this God for an idol. If we turn away from the true God and his Christ what now seems to be gold will evaporate, it will turn into ashes. All that glitters is *not* gold. Yet, if your life is just one heap of ashes God can exchange your ashes for real gold, real life. Reality. Life in Christ that is abundant, new, eternal. He can put the pieces together again, he can mend the broken heart, he can bring back meaning and purpose into your life. If you are empty, he can fill you. If there is a vacuum in your life he can give you something really worth living for.

It is also sad to note in this story of the children of Israel that they grieved not only the heart of Moses their mentor, father, friend and leader but also the heart of God:

> 'Then the Lord said to Moses, "Go down, because your people, whom you brought up out of Egypt, have become corrupt. They have been quick to turn away from what I commanded them and have made themselves an idol cast in the shape of a calf. They have bowed down to it and sacrificed to it and have said, 'These are your gods, O Israel, who brought you up out of Egypt.'
>
> "I have seen these people," the Lord said to Moses, "and they are a stiff-necked people. Now leave me alone so that my anger may burn against them and that I may destroy them. Then I will make you into a great nation."
>
> But Moses sought the favour of the Lord his God, "O Lord," he said, "why should your anger burn against your people, whom you brought out of Egypt with great power and a mighty hand? Why should the Egyptians say, 'It was with evil intent that he brought them out, to kill them in the mountains and to wipe them off the face of the earth?' Turn from your fierce anger; relent and do not bring disaster on your people. Remember your servants Abraham, Isaac and Israel, to whom you swore by your own self: " 'I will make your descendants as numerous as the stars in the sky and I will give your descendants all this land I promised them, and it will

> be their inheritance for ever.' " Then the Lord relented and did not bring on his people the disaster he had threatened.' *Exodus 37:7–14*

In spite of all they had done God did not give them up. He still commissioned Moses to go and lead them and to take them into the land which he had promised. Though they had sinned he would not break his covenant. He will keep his word. He will fulfil his promise. But in the final day of reckoning none of us gets away with presumptuous sin. Those who were led away into idolatry and gave their lives to worship on the strange altars of other gods lost out on the true purposes of God for them. Instead of becoming partners in the history of God's plan for the redemption of mankind, instead of being part of that prophetic, messianic community which eventually heralded the coming of the King, they became faint shadows and ugly memories buried in the sands of Sinai. What a complete waste!

All those who would turn away from God and worship at the altars of idolatry and materialism, in whatever shape or form, must understand that the consequences will be the same. They will lose out on the true purpose of God for their lives and, instead of being partners in the plan of God for the redemption of our world, will also become clouds which once passed this way.

Sometimes I wonder what the situation would have been like if Aaron had not taken the coward's way out. When the people demanded that he should make a god for them, instead of yielding to their pressure and giving them what they wanted he could have stood up for the Lord. He should have spoken out as a prophet in that situation, to remind them of the word of the Lord, of his ways and of his calling on their lives. Who knows? Maybe they would have stoned him or maybe they would have changed their minds and this episode would not have remained such a disgraceful chapter in the history of the people of Israel.

Even today there are many who preach what people want to hear. They give the people what they want. We bow to people pressure and, like cowards, do not have the courage to be God's prophets in today's difficult situations. We not only fail God but we fail the people. God calls us to be involved with him as partners in a divine process for the redemption of fallen humanity. Let us arise and with courage proclaim the unsearchable riches of the kingdom of God and not be ashamed of our God. Let us start *really* believing in what we believe, and with passion, conviction and courage proclaim it so that the world may know there is only one true and living God. There is only one Saviour of the world; there is no other way. There are no other gods.

MONEY AND SPIRITUALITY

When we speak of materialism it is important that we do not heap condemnation on anyone. Our aim is not to make people feel guilty because of the things they have or the position they hold. The real crux of the matter is whether or not we are faithful stewards of the things which God has permitted us to have.

The risk we run when we speak of these matters is to polarise Christians, marginalising those who are better off. We unintentionally create a division between the 'haves' and the 'have nots'.

We can create, and feed, another kind of prejudice: that between rural suburbia and the inner city church; between middle class and working class Christians. That would be silly, because we need each other. We need to seek earnestly ways of working in partnership, rather than thinking up things to accuse one another of from across the fence.

There are some important questions that we need to ask when considering how money and spirituality relate to each other.

Is true spirituality measured by how rich or poor we are?

Of course not. True spirituality flows out of our motives, our attitudes and our experience with God, and God does not judge our motives by the size of our bank balance or lack of it. True spirituality cannot be measured in commercial terms.

Is poverty a curse?

Some theologians will have us believe that poverty is a sign of God's curse, especially when they refer to the so-called third world countries. They put forward the theory that the Western world is blessed and prosperous because it is made up of Christian countries, while the third world countries are heathen. They do not prosper because the curse of God is upon them. What arrogant rubbish! Am I to understand that the blessing of God is on the West because it is Christian? *Which* Christian country? Certainly not the Western countries we know!

Even if at one time they might have embraced certain Christian principles and values, that can hardly be said of them today, though some still send out missionaries and print Bibles. The days when the West was probably known for its Christianity were the days when its countries were famous for child labour, the practice of slavery, the exploitation of coal miners, and landlords whose peasants worked for a pittance.

One needs to look at the deeper issues that cause poverty in third world countries. What about the injustices, exploitation and corruption? The lack of management skills? The western multi-nationals who devise schemes to squeeze the poorer nations? What about obsolete machinery sold to the unsuspecting third world by deceit and at enormous prices? We can safely say that just as riches are not a sign of true spirituality, poverty is not necessarily a sign of lack of spirituality or of the curse of God. Some of the greatest saints in our world are people who do not have two pennies to rub together. Who can deny the rich life of Mother Teresa? Some of the poorest people in the world have a faith that I envy, a trust that is refreshing. They have things that money cannot buy.

We are so obsessed and blinded by the spirit of materialism that we use it as a yardstick to measure the value of life. It is the god by whose standards all else is judged. This is idolatry.

Is it sinful to be rich?

Of course not. But, as Paul clearly puts it, 'the love of money is a root of all evil' (Timothy 6:9). It *is* sinful to make material things the single pursuit of our life at the expense of everything else, at the expense of our life with God, our family, friends, community. Wesley said, 'work for all you can, save all you can, give all you can.' I agree.

NEW IDOLS

How, then, can we define materialism? It is the preoccupation and obsession with wealth, things and status, especially when at the expense of people and other qualities and values. It is an insatiable thirst to acquire more. We are driven on – even if we must climb on the heads of others to get it, or run ourselves into massive debts. Materialism is when things begin to control us instead of being our servants. Material things dictate our thoughts, programmes and daily schedules. Materialism is an activity of the spirit; it feeds on the greed of men and women. It is not merely a natural, human activity; that is why I label it as idolatry. There is a spirit at work driving man towards getting, getting, getting. He is pushed into a syndrome from which he finds it very difficult to escape.

* * *

Jean is not yet thirty. She is vivacious, intelligent, hard working. She has everything to live for and there is no reason why she cannot enjoy a reasonably comfortable, happy life. Except for one thing: she is always in debt. She works hard, long hours but is never free from the heavy debt burden. She swears she does not know how she ended up in this predicament. That is the time to examine things closely. What do you find? She buys and buys on credit cards things she does not really need. She fully intends to pay, but does not take into account the amounts she has to pay in interest. Idolatry, the god of materialism, destroys.

* * *

Materialism, like other forms of idolatry, is a virus. Once it gets into the system, it grows progressively worse. Before I became a Christian, as a Hindu I worshipped idols. Our temple was filled with idols. But when I became a Christian I realised that Christ and my idols were completely incompatible. It was *either* Christ *or* my idols. I could not serve them both. I could not believe in them both. I could not be hooked by them both. I had to burn them, denounce them, destroy them. But here in the West I discover that Christians have idols of a different sort at whose altars they regularly worship. They are very modern idols: gods of science, pleasure, culture, status, sex, intellectualism. Godless universities are shrines which continue to pump out philosophies that are destroying our people and turning the nation into a godless society. Even some theologians, by their own craftiness, obscure the Jesus of the manger, the Jesus of the cross and resurrection, the Jesus of miracles. He is merely history to them, not current reality. They do not recognise their theories as the idols they are. They are too sophisticated to accept that they are idolatrous! They excuse and justify these modern idols, and clothe them with intellectual jargon, but the effect is the same. Their theories replace God in their thinking. They live by their godless theories, enshrine them and worship them.

THE NEED FOR CAUTION

There are very real dangers in not thinking carefully about our attitude to material things:

- Materialism threatens, rivals and replaces God in our lives. Can we really afford to allow mere material things to do that?
- We have an inherent tendency to shift our faith from God to things, to put our trust and our dependence on things instead of God. If we are not careful the whole ground and centre of our lives can shift from being God-dependent to things-dependent.
- Jesus clearly taught in the parable of the sower (Matthew 13) that the cares of this life and the material things of this world do strangle our growth and hinder our spirituality. The seeds of faith that God has deposited in us cannot bloom and come to full growth when the material things of life so occupy us that we have no time for God.
- Materialism promotes a life of ease and encourages a religion of convenience.
- Materialism dulls our hearing and blinds our vision. The Lord Jesus said to the church in Laodicea, 'You say, "I am rich; I have acquired wealth and do not need a thing." But you do not realise that you are wretched, pitiful, poor, blind and naked' (Revelation 3:17). Materialism tends to make us self-sufficient so we no longer feel the deep hunger after God. We no longer recognise our need to draw continually from God for our peace and joy. We also become miserable and do not always recognise how blind we can be. Our vision gets blurred, our priorities all mixed up. And often the

things we have no longer bring to us the satisfaction and fulfilment we thought they would.

It is significant that the Lord closed his exhortation to this church by saying to them, 'I stand at the door and knock. If anyone hears my voice and opens the door, I will go in and eat with him, and he with me' (Revelation 3:20). Isn't it sad that this church, which started out with such great promise, did not recognise that God was no longer in their midst? The King of glory, whom they sang to and preached about every week was no longer inside. He was outside the door of the church, he was locked out. There was no room for him in their worship. There was no room in their hearts, their activity, their scheme of things for the King of glory. Instead, they found their reason for living in the many things which they were acquiring and achieving.

• Materialism detracts from the Lordship of Christ in our lives. It drains us of our energy and time, paralyses our will and robs us of our anointing of the Holy Spirit. It leaves us with no time to wait on God to intercede and wage spiritual warfare. Even though we may claim to be spiritual Christians we are actually like dried-up sticks, like clouds without water. We are people without any real dynamism of the Holy Spirit in our lives because we have spent so much time at the altars of materialism that we have not found time to come into the inner sanctuary to dwell in the presence of God. Note the contrast: while Moses was in the presence of the Lord on the mountain, the people were dancing and singing and worshipping a golden calf in the valleys. Let us go up with Moses to the mountain top and stay there as long as it takes.

IMITATE JESUS

We need to find our pattern and example in Christ. Let us look again at the simplicity of the man from Galilee who was a friend of sinners. The poor, the prostitutes, the sick and the suffering could relate to him easily. Unfortunately, the simplicity of Christ is lost to our generation. His appeal is lost in all our religious paraphernalia and sophistication. We have become so respectable that ordinary people cannot find the real Jesus any more. We don't mirror a Christ that attracts the world, a Christ to whom the world can really relate.

Of course we need things, things to clothe us, feed us, house us; we have to look after our children and pay the bills. Nothing is wrong with that. What is wrong is that we put the cart before the horse. Jesus said, 'Seek first the Kingdom of God and his righteousness, and all these things will be given to you as well' (Matthew 6:33). We are seeking the things when we really should be seeking the Kingdom. God will look after us. We are his own children; he even knows the number of hairs on our head! He is very, very interested in us, he will not forsake us. The Lord rebuked his disciples when he said they were seeking the things that the Gentiles seek. In other words, we are no better than people without Christ. Our priorities are no different from theirs.

The Lord also said, 'Do not store up for yourselves treasures on earth . . . but store up for yourselves treasures in heaven . . . For where your treasure is, there your heart will be also' (Matthew 6:19–21).

What is your real treasure in life? In these dark times the Lord is expecting his church to fulfil its prophetic mission to this earth. So let us invest our lives in warning and winning others, and use our money and possessions to provide for the mission of the church. If we save our lives we will lose out. If we lose our lives for the sake of the kingdom we will find them again.

God is calling us to a rededication of our lives. If we take to heart the lessons from the experience of the children of Israel, and repent where we need to repent, then we could very well see the church being revitalised. It would be a church that regains something of its lost credibility and would show again the radical, prophetic edge so desperately needed if we are going to press the claims of Christ in the 1990s. God has not forsaken us. Let us awake out of our sleep and complacency, let us repent from self-centredness, self-righteousness and self-indulgence. Let us smash our idols and throw them out. Then let us dare to be all that we were redeemed to be: a holy people, a whole people, a kingdom prophetic people, a chosen race, a holy priesthood (see 1 Peter 2:9–10).

13

PIONEERS OR SETTLERS?

Israel was called to journey from Egypt through the wilderness to the Promised Land. In order to do it they had to overcome many obstacles. Those who follow Christ are also called to be pilgrims. The situation and circumstances are different but the principles are the same. We too are aliens, strangers and exiles living in a foreign country (1 Peter 2:11). We are called to journey to a city whose architect and builder is God, not to settle here. We are called to meet God at Mount Zion, rather than Sinai, and live by grace and forgiveness. We are called to be a distinctive people. We are called to be sojourners, those who travel with a sense of mission to a specified destination. We are *not* called to wander aimlessly through life with no real function or purpose.

ON THE MOVE

Pioneers must strive for excellence and pursue the highest goal with a singleness of heart. Like Paul, we must be prepared to press on and reach forward for those things which are ahead of us (Philippians 3:12–14), despising mediocrity in order that we might attain to all the fulness to which God has called us to. As the song writer has put it, 'this world is not my home, I'm just a-passing through.' We are a people in transition, on our way to a better country. We are those who have already tasted the age to come and cannot afford to be distracted. We have a date with destiny. Pioneers are not settlers!

We who follow the Lamb are citizens of a heavenly kingdom and, as such, we are called upon to change and influence the shape of things to come. While we are on the move we have a mission to the world. That mission is to reclaim all its lost territories for Christ. We must explore and expand our boundaries, conquer new areas, reach for new horizons, populate heaven by plundering hell. As New Testament pilgrim people we have an apostolic and a prophetic function to the nations of the world. There is no room for us to stagnate and go round in circles, or to get stuck in religious routines. This is a time when our dreams, our visions and the dynamism of the Spirit of God working within us should propel us forward with purpose.

COMMITTED

Like the Old Testament pioneers – Abraham, Moses, David, Daniel, Joshua, Caleb, Gideon – and the New

Testament apostles and heroes, we must accept our call and be totally committed to the cause of Christ and his Kingdom. They were captivated with a burning vision of the future and were willing to pay the price to bring it about. Sometimes they needed to be willing to lay down their lives, to be stretched beyond all human endurance and limitation in order to win their goal, the high calling of God. Pilgrim pioneers are burdened with concerns of the heart of God. Our predecessors had a look into tomorrow's world and it beckoned them to come up higher. So they blazed the trail for others to follow and laid the foundation upon which future generations could build. All this was done in very hostile environments. Can we not hear God calling us on as he did them, calling us to put our faith into action and dare to follow the Lamb wherever he leads?

The pioneering pilgrims of the Bible did not allow little things like Goliath, Pharaoh, lions, fiery furnaces, imprisonments, rivers, Jericho walls and armies to stand in their way! They went down in the annals of history as heroes of the faith. Even if they died in the attempt, they attempted! They risked their lives and reputation. They obeyed God. How about you and I taking a leaf out of their book and daring to press the battle to the gates? Daring to be pioneers rather than settlers?

PIONEERS OR SETTLERS?

Pioneers are people who secure the future by daring in the present. Settlers are those who preserve the past by venerating it and amusing themselves with past accomplishments. Pioneers are willing to take risks to become vulnerable and look silly in the eyes of people while settlers are cautious, preserving their own reputation, not willing to venture. Pioneers are people who look beyond the giants, rivers, mountains and walls and see the God of the impossible, who is able to overcome all the obstacles. Settlers measure the difficulties against their own resources and strength and clothe themselves with a grasshopper mentality. They see how impossible it is. Pioneers are people of aggressive action, willing to take bold initiatives even when it does not seem to make sense. Settlers are people of a passive, negative attitude, of debates and inaction, dotting every 'i' and crossing every 't', waiting for everything to be perfect before they attempt anything. They are the people who lose themselves in the mystery of theology, or enter into doctrinal debates and spend their lives sorting out the chronology of eschatological events.

Let us rise up as the army of God and catch a glimpse of the glory and triumphs of the crucified Lamb. Let us allow the Holy Spirit to fill us with new dynamism as we await with joyous expectation the climax of the ages and the consummation of all things in Christ. In the meantime, with holy fire burning in our hearts, let us follow our Lamb, our Lion, our servant King. Let us dare to be partners with God until we see all the kingdoms of this world become the kingdom of our God and King.

Come on pilgrims! Let us consecrate ourselves, make a new commitment of our lives and pray for something more than our yesterdays: more love, more passion, more holiness, more dynamism – more of God's supernatural power at work through us. Do not settle for less.

OTHER BOOKS IN THIS SERIES

God of New Beginnings: Matthew 1–4 in today's world (Roger Sainsbury).

Thirsty for God: Matthew 5–7: Jesus' teaching for today (Stephen Gaukroger).

Drawing Power: Living out Acts in today's world (Derek Prime).

Growing your Gifts: 2 Timothy: Ministry in today's world (Stephen Gaukroger).